Providing

Culturally

and

Linguistically

Competent

Health Care

Executive Editor: Lisa Tinoco
Project Manager: Rachel Hegarty
Production Manager: Johanna Harris
Associate Director: Cecily Pew
Executive Director: Catherine Chopp Hinckley
Joint Commission/JCR Reviewers: Michael Alcenius, Lon Berkeley, Shelby Dunster, Nancy Rollins Gantz, Marianna Grachek, Anita Guintali, Linda Hanold, Catherine Chopp Hinckley, Cecily Pew, Ila Rothchild, Amy Wilson

Joint Commission Resources Mission

The mission of Joint Commission Resources is to continuously improve the safety and quality of care in the United States and in the international community through the provision of education and consultation services and international accreditation.

Joint Commission Resources educational programs and publications support, but are separate from, the accreditation activities of the Joint Commission. Attendees at Joint Commission Resources educational programs and purchasers of Joint Commission Resources publications receive no special consideration or treatment in, or confidential information about, the accreditation process.

The inclusion of an organization name, product, or service in a Joint Commission publication should not be construed as an endorsement of such organization, product, or services, nor is failure to include an organization name, product, or service to be construed as disapproval.

This publication is designed to provide accurate and authoritative information in regard to the subject matter covered. Every attempt has been made to ensure accuracy at the time of publication, however, please note that laws, regulations and standards are subject to change. Please also note that some of the examples in this publication are specific to the laws and regulations of the locality of the facility. The information and examples in this publication are provided with the understanding that the publisher is not engaged in providing medical, legal or other professional advice. If any such assistance is desired, the services of a competent professional person should be sought.

Requests for permission to make copies of any part of this work should be mailed to:
Permissions Editor
Department of Publications
Joint Commission Resources
One Renaissance Boulevard
Oakbrook Terrace, Illinois 60181
permissions@jcrinc.com

ISBN: 0-86688-945-0

Library of Congress Control Number: 2005937110

For more information about Joint Commission Resources, please visit http://www.jcrinc.com.

Table of Contents

Chapter Four
Developing and Training Staff to be Culturally Competent   85

Chapter Five
The Business Case for Cultural and Linguistic Competence   101

Acknowledgments

Special thanks to the following people and organizations for their help in the publication of this book: Association of Professional Chaplains, Bumrungrad International, Caldwell Memorial Hospital, California Healthcare Interpreters Association (CHIA), The Commonwealth Fund, Georgetown University Child Development Center, Grantmakers in Health, Health Research and Educational Trust Program (HRET), National Association of Public Hospitals and Health Systems, and Rowan Regional Medical Center.

Special thanks also to reviewers Michael Alcenius, Lon Berkeley, Shelby Dunster, Nancy Rollins Gantz, Marianna Grachek, Anita Guintali, Linda Hanold, Catherine Chopp Hinckley, Cecily Pew, Ila Rothchild, Amy Wilson, and Rev. Sue Wintz, M.Div., BCC for their excellent contributions toward the development and publication of this book; and to David Whitaker for his diligence and patience in writing it.

Introduction

Cultural competence in health care describes the ability of systems to provide care to patients with diverse values, beliefs, and behaviors, including tailoring the delivery of health services to meet patients' physical, social, cultural, and linguistic needs. As a practice, the achievement of cultural competence means a health care system and workforce that can deliver the highest and safest quality of care to every patient, regardless of race, values, sexual orientation, religious or spiritual orientation, ethnicity, cultural background, or English proficiency.

With an increasing population growth of racial and ethnic communities and linguistic groups, each with its own cultural traits and health profiles, the health care delivery service industry in the U.S. continues to face the challenge of health disparities. Many organizations have embraced cultural and linguistic competence initiatives as a way to reflect on and respond to patients' varied perspectives, values, beliefs, and behaviors about health and well-being. In working to transcend the learned patterns of language and culture that can distinguish patient and provider in the health care setting, they are taking positive steps to make cultural competence work.

As a result, the field of "cultural competence" in health care has emerged in part to address factors that may contribute to racial and ethnic disparities in health care. A large body of published research has found that these disparities continue to exist, that racial and ethnic minorities experience a lower quality of health services and are less likely to receive even routine medical procedures than are white Americans.

Many health care experts view sociocultural differences among patients, health care providers, and, in particular, the health care system as potential causes for these disparities. These differences—which can include language barriers, differences in values and beliefs, expectations of care, and thresholds for seeking care—may influence providers' interactions and decision-making between patients in the health care delivery system.

"Cultural Competence Works" is a detailed report by the U.S. Department of Health and Human Services published in 2001 (www.hrsa.gov). It is one of many research papers, studies, and articles in recent years that have focused on the impact of cultural and linguistic competence in improving the quality of health care for diverse populations.

For health care professionals to maintain their commitment to treating the whole patient, they must possess the sensitivity, knowledge, and skills necessary to respond to the unique needs of each patient and his or her family. This book forwards the ongoing conversation on cultural and linguistic competence in health care and measures its impact on the safe provision of care. It defines the terms, outlines the practices, and shares the model approaches. It reviews the benefits, the business case, and also the barriers associated with cultural competence. In detailing the key components and recommendations for implementing cultural competent interventions, and supporting these elements with insightful case studies, this book offers health care organizations a framework of knowledge and tools on this important and emerging health initiative.

*T*ERMINOLOGY

Cultural and linguistic competence is "the ability of health care providers and institutions to deliver effective services to racially, ethnically, and culturally diverse patient populations."[1]

Chapter One, "Language and its Effect on the Safe Provision of Care," takes a closer look at language barriers in health care and the impact that cultural and linguistic competence can make in eliminating those barriers. It outlines the demographics, disparities, and medical consequences associated with caring for those with limited English proficiency. In assessing the literacy levels of this population, this chapter examines the communications strategies of health care organizations and considers the costs and benefits of medical interpretation services and staff hiring and training. It also considers the steps ahead, and the potential of partnerships committed to ensuring that all patients receive equal access to quality health care.

Chapter Two, "Overcoming Health Barriers Through Cultural Competence," delves into the concepts of culture and the practices of cultural competence, and considers the effect that misconceptions can have on medical viewpoints. In defining key terms, this chapter also discusses the health disparities linked to cultural barriers between patient and provider. The chapter outlines strategies of cultural assessment, provides a self–assessment tool, and looks at the unique challenges of an international hospital.

Chapter Three, "The Role of Community in Cultural Competence," looks at the interrelationship of community and cultural competence. It explores the methods and benefits of involving individuals and institutions in health care programs and the importance of health promotion to the community. This chapter also describes the ways in which hiring and training can strengthen ties with the community, and outlines the pivotal process of collecting data from the community to better respond to its health care needs.

Chapter Four, "Developing and Training Staff to be Culturally Competent," looks at the broad practices of cultural competence and medical interpretation training and reveals great progress and serious challenges. This chapter reviews the variety of training approaches and programming, outlines the settings and services, examines training curricula and methods of measurement, considers the contribution of health care leaders to effective training, and assesses the need to standardize training methodologies.

Chapter Five, "The Business Case for Cultural and Linguistic Competence," considers how the forces of change in health care have affected the emergence of cultural competence as a viable intervention, and whether these forces support the case of cultural competence as a viable investment in the business of health care. In defining the business case for cultural competence, this chapter examines the incentives of achieving quality care and cost effectiveness. It looks at the role of leadership in recognizing and promoting the financial rewards of cultural competence and, finally, it considers both the challenges and promise of cultural competence as a business strategy in the years ahead.

Reference

1. Bigby J. (ed.): *Cross Cultural Medicine*. Philadelphia: American College of Physicians, 2003.

One

Language and its Effect on the Safe Provision of Care

A Vietnamese-speaking patient is unable to schedule a follow-up appointment for an abnormal mammogram because the receptionist only speaks English. As a result, treatment and necessary procedures are delayed.

A Chinese-speaking woman visits her primary care physician complaining of a mass in her wrist. Luckily, this physician is able to speak the patient's language and communicate effectively. She is referred for a biopsy and returns to the same physician several weeks later for a follow-up appointment. The patient tells her physician that the surgery was performed, but she does not know what the surgeon found. She also mentions that she was prescribed medications, but has stopped taking them because she felt fine. Her physician examines the bottles and discovers the medications are for tuberculosis. The patient is not aware of this diagnosis. More alarming, she is not aware the disease can be spread easily to others and that effective treatment includes taking her medications for one year.

A call from the mother and sister of a Spanish-speaking man reported that he was "intoxicado." Paramedics and the hospital personnel incorrectly interpreted this as intoxicated or drunk and, therefore, left him alone, offering no treatment. It turned out the man was actually having a stroke, and this mistake resulted in him being paralyzed. After settling out of court, the health care institution was required to pay $71 million.

A Mien-speaking man with chronic hepatitis is referred to a gastroenterologist for a biopsy of his liver. Through a Mien interpreter, he reported back to the referring physician that a staff member yelled at him for not bringing his own interpreter. After multiple frustrating encounters, the patient asked to be referred to another doctor, a bold act for someone whose culture does not normally allow for questioning of a physician's authority.

> A Spanish-speaking patient presenting chest pain, unrelated to coronary artery disease, is scheduled for multiple unnecessary diagnostic procedures due to the inability of the medical team to get a good history.[1]

Language is often the point at which the patient and provider meet. It is the method with which patients are introduced to the health system, report their conditions, learn of their options, and make decisions about their treatment. But, as the examples above reveal, when patients and providers do not speak the same language or share the same understanding of values and beliefs related to health care, this method is not always clear and this meeting is not always successful. What is lost in translation has emerged as a barrier to quality care.

This chapter takes a closer look at the ways in which language barriers affect the provision of care, and the impact that cultural and linguistic competence can make in eliminating those barriers. It outlines the demographics, disparities, and medical consequences associated with caring for those with limited English proficiency. In assessing the literacy levels of this population, this chapter examines the communications strategies of health care organizations and considers the costs and benefits of medical interpretation services and staff hiring and training. It also considers the steps ahead, and the potential of partnerships committed to ensuring that all patients receive equal access to quality health care.

TERMINOLOGY

A patient is an individual who receives care, treatment, and services.

Within different types of health care organizations, a variety of synonyms are available for the word patient, including client, resident, consumer, customer, and care recipient. In this book, to prevent confusion and ensure consistency, the term patient will be used throughout to represent any individual served within a health care organization.

Identifying the Demographics of and Disparities Caused by Language Barriers

With more than 46 million people in the United States who do not speak English as their primary language, and more than 21 million people who speak English less than "very well,"[2] language is recognized as a significant barrier to quality health care.[3] During the last 20 years, the U.S. has experienced a dramatic increase in the number of immigrants from Mexico and various countries from Latin America and Asia. In the 1990s, according to the U.S. Census, the foreign-born population nearly doubled to 31 million, or 11% of the 281 million people that constitute the U.S. population. Of the total foreign-born population, 51% were born in Latin America and 25.5% were born in Asia. In June of 2005, the U.S. Census Bureau reported that Hispanics accounted for half of the 2.9 million U.S. population growth from 2003 to 2004 and now constitute one-seventh of all people in the U.S. The Census Bureau estimated that 41.3 million Hispanics live in the U.S.

When both citizens and noncitizens are combined, it is estimated that nearly 25 million adults encounter language barriers when they receive health care. This is one factor that contributes to what has been termed health disparity.[4]

Several recent studies have documented evidence from the last 20 years showing that racial, ethnic, and language-based disparities remain present in health care. According to The Institute of Medicine (IOM) report "Unequal Treatment: Confronting Racial and Ethnic Disparities in Health Care,"[5] issued in 2002, "The sources of these disparities are complex, are rooted in historic and contemporary inequities, and involve many participants at several levels, including health systems, their administrative and bureaucratic processes, utilization managers, health care professionals, and patients."

𝒯ERMINOLOGY

Health disparity, as defined by the Health Resources and Service Administration (HRSA), is a population-specific difference in the presence of disease, health outcomes, or access to care. Language barriers between patients and health care providers may affect all three outcomes (that is, disease incidence, health outcomes, access to care).[4]

Finding Evidence of Disparities, and Their Defining Characteristics

Language is just one factor that contributes to health disparities. Stereotyping, biases, and prejudice on the part of health care providers can all contribute to unequal treatment. With the pressures of time, cost containment, and cognitive complexity, the conditions in which many encounters take place may enhance the likelihood that these processes will result in care poorly matched to the needs of minority patients.[5]

In accessing care, minorities may also experience obstacles related to cultural familiarity and geography, even when insured at the same level as whites. Financial and institutional arrangements of health systems, as well as the legal, regulatory, and policy environment in which they operate, may also have disparate and negative effects on minorities' ability to attain quality care. While disparities associated with socioeconomic differences tend to diminish and, in a few cases, disappear altogether when socioeconomic factors are controlled, the majority of studies find that racial and ethnic disparities remain even after adjustment for socioeconomic differences and other health care access–related factors.[5]

Considering the Characteristics of Those with Language Barriers

To examine the relationship of language barriers and health disparities, it is necessary to understand the characteristics of those for whom language is an obstacle. Only a few studies conducted in the U.S. agree that certain demographic factors are associated with the level of English proficiency across races and ethnicities. Looking at a total of 4,380 adults continuously enrolled in an HMO for two years, one study's descriptive data indicated that those who did not speak English well enough were significantly older and poorer.[4] This study also found that more women than men tended to have severe language barriers. Another study revealed that Latinos with limited English proficiency (LEP) were older than Latinos with better English proficiency, and that Latinos with LEP were more likely to be female and to be less literate than English speakers of all ethnicities.[4]

TERMINOLOGY

Limited English proficiency (LEP) describes persons who have difficulty speaking, reading, writing, or understanding the English language because they are individuals who

- were not born in the United States or whose primary language is a language other than English; or
- come from environments where a language other than English is dominant; or
- are American Indian and Alaskan Natives and who come from environments where a language other than English has had a significant impact on their level of English language proficiency; and
- by reason, thereof, are denied the opportunity to learn successfully in classrooms where the language of instruction is English or to participate fully in American society.[6]

Some groups of Asians, such as Japanese, are an exception to the characteristics previously described because they tend to be similar to non-Hispanic whites in socioeconomic status. Still, Japanese clients also identify language as the most difficult and obvious obstacle to accessing health care in the U.S.[7] and many Asians share similar disadvantages as Latinos when it comes to language barriers.[8] Language barriers, regardless of socioeconomic status, are an independent factor that negatively affects access to care.

Some studies describe behavior due to cultural beliefs without clearly differentiating it from behavior due to language barriers. Culturally specific health beliefs and behaviors must be considered separately from barriers related to language. In other words, the use of translators does not in itself decrease barriers to care.[4]

Assessing the Consequences of Unequal Care

Language barriers are associated with lack of awareness about health care benefits (such as Medicaid eligibility),[9] less insured status, longer visit time per clinic visit, less frequent clinic visits, less understanding of the physicians' explanations, more emergency room visits, less follow-up, and less satisfaction with health services.[4] The personal stories of those who have encountered these barriers illustrate the consequences of these findings and the reality of the system.

A 47-year-old man was found to have advanced lung cancer. After discussing options with his primary care physician, the patient decided in favor of palliative care. His physician referred him for home hospice. Two months later the patient's brother called because the patient had been having intractable pain. Because the patient had lost his insurance, home hospice had rejected the referral and sent him to a social worker, who gave the patient a Medicaid application. Neither the patient nor his brother had been able to read or complete the form. The brother eventually submitted the form with the assistance of the physician. Two weeks after the patient died, his brother received a letter informing him that the patient had qualified for Medicaid.[10]

One section of a report by Grantmakers in Health, entitled "In the Right Words: Addressing Language and Culture in Providing Health Care,"[1] reviews the ramifications of poor linguistic access. Please see Sidebar 1-1. Health Consequences of Language Barriers Access on pages 14 and 15.

This body of research indicates that speaking a language other than English puts a patient at risk for adverse health outcomes and reduced quality of care. The Institute of Medicine (IOM) "Unequal Treatment" report suggests that factors within the health care system can exert different effects on patients, resulting in negative consequences for those with limited English proficiency. The report also noted that "language mismatches are a fertile soil for racial and ethnic disparities in care."

Recognizing Literacy Levels Among an Organization's Patients

More than 90 million Americans are either functionally illiterate or unable to read above a fifth-grade level, yet most patient information material is written at a tenth-grade reading level or higher and much of it is peppered with medical jargon and terminology that reflects an increasingly complex health care system.[11]

𝒯ERMINOLOGY

Health literacy is defined as the degree to which people have the capacity to obtain, process, and understand basic health information and services needed to make appropriate health decisions.[12]

More simply put, health literacy is an individual's ability to understand health care information—such as instructions regarding prescriptions, informed consent documents, health information sheets, and insurance forms—and to use that information to make decisions about one's health care. The implications of low health literacy for our nation's health care system are staggering. According to the U.S. Department of Adult Education, poor health literacy can lead to the improper use of medication, rehospitalization, birth defects, incurable cancer that could have been detected earlier if the patient had understood its seriousness and implications, and other problems. The cost of low health literacy in human suffering is immeasurable.

Sidebar 1-1.
Health Consequences of Language Barriers Access

Language barriers have been shown to impede access at several entry points, from having health insurance to receiving basic and preventive care to accessing specialty services. In a study of the effect of English language proficiency on enrollment of Medicaid-eligible children in publicly funded health insurance programs, most families with eligible children reported not knowing eligibility guidelines and difficulty translating enrollment forms as reasons for not enrolling in the program.[9] In a nationwide telephone study of insured adults, Spanish-speaking Latinos were significantly less likely than non-Latino whites to have had a physician visit, flu shot, or mammogram in the preceding year. To isolate the role of language, non-Latino whites were then compared to English-speaking Latinos. The study found no difference in utilization, which points to language as the driving force for this disparity in access to preventive services.

Patient Comprehension

After LEP patients get into the system, language barriers may compromise comprehension of diagnosis, treatment instructions, and plans for follow-up care. At the same time, language concordance—when the physician and patient speak the same language—has been associated with better patient self-reported physical functioning, psychological well being, and health perceptions, as well as lower pain levels.

Patient Satisfaction

Patients are more satisfied when they have access to a trained and qualified interpreter.

In one study, 32% of those who needed an interpreter, but did not get one, said they would not return to the hospital if they became insured, while only 9% of those who did receive an interpreter said they would not return.[13] Another study—comparing LEP versus English-speaking Asian and Hispanic patients—found significantly worse reports of care on multiple domains, including timeliness of care, provider communication, staff helpfulness, and plan service.[14] Oftentimes, satisfaction with care at a particular institution determines whether a patient will return for subsequent care at the same institution, if given a choice.

(continued)

Sidebar 1-1.
(continued)

Quality of Care

Language barriers diminish quality of care and can lead to serious complications and adverse clinical outcomes. One study found that patients with a language barrier were more likely to have self-reported outpatient drug complications. They were also more likely to have a number of other problems, such as hospitalizations and lower medication compliance. When a prescribing physician is unable to communicate effectively with his or her patient, serious side effects can occur if an accurate history is not taken.[15]

Costs to the Health Care System

Language barriers can escalate costs to the health care system by increasing inefficiencies and unnecessary testing. When treating LEP patients, providers often order additional tests and other costly—and sometimes invasive—procedures for fear of missing a diagnosis when a good history would have sufficed. The practice is so common it has come to be characterized as "veterinary medicine." In the absence of verbal communication, test results, visual assessment of symptoms, and hand motions must form the basis of a diagnosis. These add up to unnecessary costs to the health care system. A study in a Chicago pediatric emergency department documented the cost of language barriers. After controlling for severity of illness, vital signs, tests, and insurance status, the investigators found that visits that had a language barrier were on the average $38 more expensive and required an average of 20 minutes longer than those without language barriers.[16]

Source: Grantmakers in Health: In the right words: Addressing language and culture in providing health care. Issue brief no. 18: 5–8, 2003. Used with permission.

Assessing the Awareness of Health Literacy

In recent years the issue of health literacy has become a significant issue for U.S. Surgeon General Richard A. Carmona, M.D., who said, "Low health literacy is a threat to the health and well-being of Americans and the well-being of the American medical system." Statistics presented by the surgeon general at a June 2003 address to the AMA's House of Delegates concluded the fact that low health literacy costs the health care industry more than $73 billion a year in misdirected or misunderstood services.[17]

Still, a 2003 survey from the AMA Foundation found that two-thirds of the physicians questioned said they had not heard of health literacy. Of those who had heard of it, 87% agreed that it was "very important" and "very necessary" for proper health care, and 67% said they wanted to make changes in their offices to address health literacy.[17]

I P

Enhanced patient-provider communication will lead to more effective diagnosis, which can reduce the need for unnecessary testing and more aggressive treatment. Improved communication about publicly funded programs will also improve access to care for eligible patients, as well as provide new funding streams for hospitals and health systems treating these patients.[1]

"I think when we call it health literacy, we stumble because we think it is just about those who cannot read," said Robert Friedland, the founding director of the Center on an Aging Society at Georgetown University, in an article entitled "Putting the Spotlight on Health Literacy to Improve Quality Care."[17] "I think that is a mistake because there are people who can read but they have the inability to put that information together because it requires a [variety] of skills—not just reading but also [understanding] instructions and visual cues and having empowerment to just ask questions."

Illustrating this point, testimony heard by the Committee on Health Literacy and the IOM in 2004 included a college administrative assistant who reported she did not understand the dosage information on her medicine and, as a result, fell ill and had to be hospitalized. A filmmaker and world traveler told the committee that she had difficulty reading five pages of hospital consent forms and only after surgery found out she had had a hysterectomy. And, a man with a chronic heart condition said he could not decipher words such as angioplasty that were frequently used by his caregivers. All three of these patients are primary English speakers.[18]

According to Ruth Parker, an associate professor of medicine at the Emory University School of Medicine, one reason the problem is underestimated is because many people are very good at concealing their lack of comprehension. This can result in emotional and spiritual distress, thus hindering the interaction even more if the health care providers are unaware of these dynamics and how to respond to them. "I think people hide it because it is so embarrassing to have to admit you do not know," said Parker in the "Putting the Spotlight on Health Literacy to Improve Quality Care" article. Another reason is that many doctors are reluctant to simplify their presentations because they fear their patients will think they are talking down to them. "I think from a system standpoint, we have to realize that one of the reasons we do not know [the extent of the literacy problem] has to do with how we are," Parker said. "So it is going to involve a cultural shift on the part of providers."

Promoting Health Literacy Through Partnerships

One aspect of that cultural shift in health care demands that organizations find ways to partner with the community to figure out where intervention problems exist. Partnerships and cooperative efforts, according to Parker, can be used to "bridge the enormous gap that is being created by the fact that those that are providing health care and those who are in need of service very commonly do not share a common language and understanding."[17]

One could argue that accountability lies with the patient. In the past, health care organizations have labeled patients who did not follow the instructions given to them by their providers as "noncompliant." If patients cannot follow instructions because they cannot understand them, however, accusing them of noncompliance is unfair.[11]

Business Sense for Promoting Health Literacy

Studies have determined that patients who do not understand and therefore cannot follow treatment protocols add cost to the system.

Operationally, it makes good business sense for health care organizations to improve the health literacy of its patients. But health care executives also have an obligation to attend to the best interests of everyone served by their organization.

With even well-educated people finding it difficult to understand what is written in legal and medical jargon, some experts have suggested that if people make unhealthy choices based on unreadable information, such information may be unethical because it takes away the ability of patients to make truly informed choices.[18] Patients will not make informed decisions if they cannot understand the information they have received.

Some patient advocates suggest that health care organizations route resources into literacy programs to ensure that every child grows into an adult who can read at a tenth-grade level. While partnering with communities in supporting literacy programs is an effective long-term solution, it fails to address a health care system that is currently serving a significant number of adult patients who cannot understand health care information.[11]

Altering Communication Materials to Address Health Literacy

Organizations can provide easy-to-understand materials to all their patients by modifying their own health information. Whether the message is conveyed in printed brochures, over the Internet, or in conversation, organizations can communicate more effectively with patients if those messages are communicated at a lower education level. In

 I P
Although simple literacy tests exist, conducting them in the health care setting is unnecessary if an organization treats all patients by providing easy-to-understand and easy-to-use materials.

producing brochures, signs, and forms in clear, simple language—and speaking to patients in a similar manner—organizations will reduce the discrepancies between patient readability levels.

Although most people understand the words "bleeding," "high blood pressure," and "cancer," not everyone understands "hemorrhage," "hypertension," and "carcinoma." Sidebar 1-2. Creating Easy-to-Read Materials on page 18 offers several tips for creating more effective communication materials.

As mentioned, modifications that simplify written materials can also be adapted to oral communication between provider and patient.

I P

If organizations modify patient communication materials to a lower education level, they should avoid using medical jargon by making sure that words used between providers and patients are straightforward and simple.

Analyzing the Readability of Communication Material

Organizations such as the Institute for Healthcare Advancement provide resources that can help health care organizations evaluate the reading level of their patient communication materials. A readability analysis, such as the Suitability Assessment of Materials (SAM), involves both writers and readers of materials that a typical patient or employee might receive to assess whether such documents are consistently readable. Table 1-1. Readability Analysis of Sample Documents on page 19 illustrates the scoring process for these documents.[18]

In addition to performing a readability analysis on materials, organizations should consider talking with everyone involved in the writing and editing process as well as the patients and employees who are expected to read those materials.

Sidebar 1-2. Creating Easy-to-Read Materials

Linda McIntosh of the Cambridge Health Alliance has compiled tips to make written material easier for patients to understand. She suggests using materials—often labeled "easy to read" or "plain language"—that have most of the following characteristics:

- Lots of white space on a page
- Pictures that explain the content and reflect the intended audience
- Short paragraphs, short sentences, easy words
- Personal words ("you" rather than "the patient")
- Active verbs
- Need-to-know information—not everything about a topic
- Content in a logical order

When only hard-to-read material is available, McIntosh suggests that providers can

- Review handouts with patients
- Identify the most important parts of the material (highlighting them in yellow)
- Draw a small image next to text as a memory jogger
- Make a brief audiotape with critical information for patients

Source: Simmons J.C. (ed.): Putting the spotlight on health literacy to improve quality care. *The Quality Letter for Healthcare Leaders* 15(7): 9, 2003. Used with permission.

Strategies to Eliminate Problematic
Health Care Terms

In 2002 The Partnership for Clear Health Communication, an advocacy group addressing the challenges of low health literacy, launched an educational campaign promoting clear health communication between providers and patients. Called "Ask Me 3," the campaign urges patients to ask three simple but essential questions for everyday health care:

1. What is my problem?
2. What do I need to do?
3. Why is it important for me to do that?[17]

T I P
Using illustrations in patient communication materials can also increase patient comprehension, especially among low-literate populations.

The aim of the three-question strategy is to destigmatize the embarrassment surrounding low health literacy and give providers a cue to deliver explanations of complex health information by breaking them down into three clear and concise messages.

Table 1-1. Readability Analysis of Sample Documents

Sample Document	Grade Level	SAM Score	Readers Easy	Readers Hard	Writers Easy	Writers Hard
Admission Forms	—	—	—	—	—	—
Employee Benefits						
Summary Plan Description	—	—	—	—	—	—
Retirement Plan	—	—	—	—	—	—
Informed Consent Forms						
Admission	—	—	—	—	—	—
Typical Procedure	—	—	—	—	—	—
Clinical Trials	—	—	—	—	—	—
Health Information						
Brochures	—	—	—	—	—	—
Hospital Bill	—	—	—	—	—	—
Patient Rights						
State Bill of Rights	—	—	—	—	—	—
Federal Patient Rights	—	—	—	—	—	—
HIPAA Notice	—	—	—	—	—	—
Quarterly Newsletter	—	—	—	—	—	—
Web site	—	—	—	—	—	—
Online Privacy Info	—	—	—	—	—	—
Online Terms of Serv	—	—	—	—	—	—
Average:	—	—	__%	__%	__%	__%

Reprinted with the permission of Aspen Publishers from Hochhauser M.: Is it ethical to give out unreadable information? *Managed Care Quarterly* 11(2): 34-36, 2003.

To promote better understanding between patients and providers, "Ask Me 3" has also developed four categories of health care words that can cause misunderstandings and has suggested alternative words or phrases to make the meanings clearer to patients. Their wordplay has been adapted on page 21 in Sidebar 1-3. Making Health Care Words Understandable for All.

 I P
Better communication results when those involved in writing health care materials make a habit of talking with those expected to read those materials.

People are sensitive to being deceived by language. Clear communication is basic to any trusting relationship. If people cannot understand an organization's materials, they may wonder how much the organization can be trusted. Organizations should also question how findings from their communications audit apply to the organization's mission. By saying one thing but doing another, organizations will at the very least create confusion among patients and employees.[18]

Enhancing Personal Communication to Address Health Literacy

Help your staff develop patient communication skills through ongoing education. Emphasize that these skills include leading clinical conversations that are not rushed, are without condescension, and take into account particular views, beliefs, or circumstances of a patient or a patient's family. Health care providers should reinforce all written messages verbally.

I P
On each document being distributed, organizations should state at the top of page one how to seek further assistance if anything in the document is difficult to comprehend.

This initiative, often referred to as "teach-backs," is one in which doctors and clinicians ask patients to explain a diagnosis or treatment in their own words. They also ask patients exactly how they plan to take their medication. Health care staff should understand that jargon such as "take when you awaken" or "take with food" may be misinterpreted.[11] Some health care providers offer additional verbal resources to patients, such as a 24-hour toll-free number to assist them with any questions or concerns about their conditions or treatments.

Using Medical Interpretation Services to Improve Quality of Care

To build a healthy partnership between LEP patients and health care providers, many organizations rely on the help of a medical interpreter. A report by the Center for Community Health Research and Action at Brandeis University revealed that more than one-fourth of limited-English patients without interpreters did not understand medication instructions.[19]

While previous work has shown that family members and untrained bilingual nurses who provide ad hoc interpretation can commit many errors of interpretation,[3] many

Sidebar 1-3.
Making Health Care Words Understandable for All

Medical Word Examples
(words often used by physicians and in health care instructions)

Problem Word	Consider Using
Ailment	Sickness, illness, problem with your health
Benign	Will not cause harm; is not cancer
Condition	How you feel; health problem
Dysfunction	Problem; something not working well
Inhibitor	Drug that stops something that is bad for you
Intermittent	Off and on
Lesion	Wound; sore; infected patch of skin
Oral	By mouth
Procedure	Something done to treat your problem; operation
Vertigo	Dizziness

Concept Word Examples
(words used to describe an idea or notion)

Problem Word	Consider Using
Active role	Taking part in
Avoid	Stay away from; do not use (or eat)
Collaborate	Work together
Factor	Other thing
Gauge	Measure; get a better idea of; test (depending on context)
Intake	What you eat or drink; what goes in your body
Landmark	Very important (as adjective); important event or turning point (as noun)
Option	Choice; more than one way
Referral	Ask you to see another doctor; get a second opinion
Wellness	Good health; feeling good

(continued)

Sidebar 1-3. *(continued)*

Category Word Examples

(words describing a group or subset that may be unfamiliar)

Problem Word	*Consider Using*
Activity	Something you do or do often, such as driving a car
Adverse (reaction)	Bad
Cognitive	Learning; thinking
Hazardous	Not safe; dangerous
High-intensity	Use an example, such as running exercise
Generic	Product sold without a brand name
Noncancerous	Not cancer; does not have cancer
Poultry	Chicken, turkey, and so on
Prosthesis	Replacement for a body part; replace a part of the body with something
Support	Help with your needs, such as through money, friendship, or care

Value Judgment Word Examples

(words that may need a visual or other example to convey their meaning clearly)

Problem Word	*Consider Using*
Adequate	Enough *Example:* "adequate water"—6 to 9 glasses a day
Adjust	Fine tune; change
Cautiously	With care; slowly
Excessive	Too much *Example:* "bleeding"—if blood soaks through the bandage
Increase gradually	Add to *Example:* "exercise"—add 5 minutes per week
Moderately	Not too much *Example:* "exercise"—so you do not get out of breath
Progressive	Gets worse or better
Routinely	Often *Example:* every week, every other day
Significantly	Enough to make a difference
Temporary	For a limited time *Example:* for less than a week, for less than a day

Source: Simmons J.C. (ed.): Putting the spotlight on health literacy to improve quality care. *The Quality Letter for Healthcare Leaders* 15(7): 10–11, 2003. Used with permission.

organizations continue to avoid the cost of hiring full-time interpreters and the rising cost of telephonic interpreter services (an audio interpretation device) by training existing staff members to do the job.

Using Staff as Medical Interpreters

A hospital center in an ethnically diverse community in Queens, New York, serves as one example of an organization turning to its own employees to fill the void of medical interpretation.[20] In this facility, it was not uncommon to see hospital workers combing staff lounges for interpreters of various languages. The hospital formed translation teams drawn from their nurses, clerks, orderlies, housekeepers, and counselors with fluency in at least one foreign language. A specialist in training medical interpreters trained more than 100 staff as medical interpreters in languages that include Bengali, Urdu, Hindi, and Haitian Creole.

> ### TIP
> Organizations should consider strategies that encourage patients to ask questions, including providing patients with written materials that prompt them to seek further information from health care staff. The Joint Commission's Speak Up campaign encourages patients to become informed and active members of the health care team. For more information, please visit the Joint Commission Web site at http://www.jcaho.org and click on the Speak Up link under "Top Spots."

A health care organization treating patients of so many different languages is certainly unique. With a rapidly growing Hispanic population in the U.S., medical staff working in virtually every part of the country will encounter patients whose primary language is Spanish. At best, an inability to communicate with these patients is inconvenient and frustrating; at worst, it compromises care.[21]

Finding and training bilingual staff members who can help an organization create a welcoming environment in which non–English-speaking patients feel comfortable disclosing their personal information can be a challenge.

TERMINOLOGY
Medical interpretation is the ability to interpret the spoken conversation between provider and client within the medical context, with a specific emphasis on the ability to use and explain medical terms in both languages.[19]

Training Staff as Medical Interpreters

Organizations should develop a comprehensive strategy in training staff members as medical interpreters. They can begin by considering a plan that follows the eight general rules listed in Table 1-2. Eight Rules for Medical Interpreters on pages 25–27.

Relying on Professional Medical Interpreters

Although it is clear that errors in medical interpretation frequently have clinical consequences, some studies have found that ad hoc interpreters are significantly more likely to commit errors of potentially critical consequence than professional medical interpreters.[19]

Risks are involved in relying on family members or volunteers to serve as the go-between for doctor—or other staff member—and patient. Patients often will not provide their doctor with sensitive information through relatives.

Filtering information through family or friends can be detrimental to medical staff and patients alike, and can lead to public health problems. One example involves a Spanish-speaking pregnant woman who entered a hospital emergency room. In triage, a family member who spoke little English assisted her, but he did not repeat all the questions asked by the nurse. The hospital later learned the woman suffered from active tuberculosis, but only after several hospital staff members were exposed.[20] A trained medical interpreter could have possibly prevented such a problem.

> ***T*IP**
> Organizations have found that bilingual staff members, if properly trained to fill the role, can be effective in comforting and communicating with non–English-speaking patients.[21]

Hiring and Training Staff in Linguistic Competence

The ideal environment of overcoming language barriers in a health care setting is one that depends on the effectiveness of professional interpreters, but the lack of diversity in the health care workforce is also a broad issue relevant to language access.[1] Increasing the representation of bilingual/bicultural providers is an essential complement to the need to increase the availability of trained medical interpreters.

Several health plans now publish the language of their providers in their provider directories, but there is no standardization as to the accuracy of those self-declarations. Providers may list the languages they speak or those spoken by anyone employed in their office, but oftentimes it is without further questioning. With an aim to enhance its services and accountability, organizations can conduct a detailed language survey of their provider network, with questions such as Where did you learn the language? Are you a native speaker? Did you learn it in high school? Did you enter medical/professional school speaking that language?[19]

> ***T*IP**
> Trained medical interpreters are not only better able to communicate medical terms but can also reduce the ever-present risk of breaching patient privacy and confidentiality.

Benefiting from Bilingual Staff Members

Language needs extend beyond the examination room. It is important to develop the language skills of others in the health care organization because, during their visit, patients

Table 1-2.
Eight Rules for Medical Interpreters

1. **Use the universal form of the language whenever possible.** Regional words and meanings may be confusing or misleading to patients, regardless of what language they speak. Many languages have a universal or "high" form of the language that is free of regional words and dialects and can be understood by native speakers from all regions. Using universal Spanish with non–English-speaking Hispanic patients can minimize confusion and increase comprehension. Using the universal form of the language is especially important when patients are from a different region or country than the staff member doing the interpreting.

2. **Refrain from assuming the role of interviewer or decision maker.** Instead, the interpreting staff member should encourage and help maintain conversation between the physician—or another member of the interdisciplinary team—and patient.

3. **Let the patient lead the discussion.** In general, it is best to let the patient direct the flow of conversation. The staff member doing the interpreting should refrain from interrupting the patient, other than asking him or her to slow down or pause for a moment for the interpreter to bring the physician—or other health care team member—into the conversation. The interpreter should encourage the patient to bring up topics of concern in the order the patient chooses. By allowing the patient to start the encounter with the topic of his or her choice, the interpreter helps center the encounter around the patient's needs and provides the patient/family with a sense of control in the interaction, which can lower anxiety and increase compliance. If during the encounter the patient changes the topic, the interpreter should be careful not to ignore the patient's comments. Additionally, at the end of each segment of the history, the interpreter should ask the patient if there is anything else he or she would like to discuss with the physician or another member of the health care team. If the patient expresses his or her opinion, the interpreter should translate it exactly to that team member, even if the interpreter does not agree with it. If the team member asks the patient to make a decision about something, the interpreter should not try to influence that decision.

4. **Translate everything.** Extra conversation between the interpreting staff member and the patient or physician that is not interpreted to the other party can lead to miscommunication and subsequent errors. The interpreter may need to ask the patient or physician to clarify what he or she is saying so the interpreter understands the context of the conversation. Conveying the content of what was said does not necessarily require word-for-word translation. However, if the interpreter does not relay all the information from the patient to the physician and vice versa, then the lost information can lead to medical errors. The interpreter needs to convey everything that was said without additions, deletions, or changes to the meaning.

(continued)

Table 1-2.
(continued)

5. **Be aware of culturally significant issues that affect patient care, and translate in a way that conveys the cultural framework.** The staff member doing the interpreting should try to explain things to the patient and the physician in a way that communicates the cultural context of the conversation. For example, a patient from a matriarchal culture might not want to take a certain medication because it would be costly and would not please his or her mother. Rather than assume that the physician understands the cultural context, the interpreter should translate that concern in such a way that the physician understands why the mother is such an important figure to the patient. An interpreter's training should include effective ways to identify, understand, and communicate a patient's beliefs and values or know who within the interdisciplinary team needs to be asked to do so, such as a staff chaplain. Interpreters also need to be aware of their own beliefs and values, and be careful not to apply them to patients or families when they are interpreting for the members of the health care team.

6. **Meet the patient prior to the medical encounter.** Frequently patients do not recognize that the staff member doing the interpreting is an integral part of their health care and they are uncomfortable sharing information with the interpreter. Gender differences can compound this discomfort. For example, in his initial visit a 39-year-old Hispanic man with painful lesions on his buttocks stated that the lesions had been hurting for three weeks and had worsened to the point of intolerable pain when sitting or lying down. When questioned at the follow-up visit, the patient admitted that the lesions had been present intermittently for approximately nine years, with two exacerbations of symptoms in the last four years. He was subsequently diagnosed with perianal fistulas and referred for surgical evaluation and treatment. When asked what kept him from sharing this information initially, he answered that he was uncomfortable disclosing this information to a female interpreter. Instead of volunteering information, he answered only the exact questions asked. In hindsight, having the patient meet the staff person prior to the medical encounter would have given the staff member an opportunity to formalize his or her role in the patient's health care and might may have made the patient more comfortable.

7. **Develop interpreter-physician work plans for each patient.** While the patient should be allowed to direct the topics of conversation, the physician, multidisciplinary team member, and the staff member doing the interpreting should agree on the structure of the interaction prior to the visit. Having an individualized work plan increases your ability to identify and meet the needs and expectations of each patient. Developing these plans requires only a few minutes of discussion prior to entering the exam room. Take, for example, a patient with diabetes. Prior to the visit, a physician might tell the interpreter that he plans to begin by having the patient share any recent concerns

(continued)

Table 1-2.
(continued)

related to her diabetes. After those are addressed, he will then provide some counseling. However, the patient has a history of noncompliance because she often does not have enough money to purchase her medication. If this is the case today, the physician explains that they will drop the planned visit structure and will instead spend the rest of the visit on getting her social assistance. It is important that the staff member be aware of the resources available to help assist with this and to be sure that the referral is made to the appropriate person.

8. **Seek continuing education.** Even without formal interpretation training, bilingual staff members can learn to do most of the things mentioned above. To improve their interpretation skills, however, they should participate in educational programs, and physicians and organizations should encourage this. The Cross Cultural Health Care Program (http://www.xculture.org/index.cfm) offers a variety of educational resources. For a list of resources by state, visit the National Council on Interpreting in Health Care's Web site at http://www.ncihc.org/hciaus.aspx. Ongoing training is important not only for increasing job satisfaction but also for improving quality of care and service within your practice.

All these suggestions should be reviewed by the organization and modified to meet its unique needs.

Source: Sevilla Matir J.F., Willis D.R.: Using bilingual staff members as interpreters. *Family Practice Management* 11(7): 34–36, 2004. Used with permission.

interact with staff including receptionists, orderlies, lab technicians, chaplains, social workers, housekeepers, transporters, and pharmacists, among others. Organizations tend to forget the impact "untrained" staff members can have on patient care. Bilingual/bicultural providers can gain insight into the patient's culture, and the ability to speak to the patient directly can help build a connection between provider and patient that includes having a mutual understanding of cultural beliefs and health care practices and attitudes.[1]

The advantages of having providers who speak their patients' languages plays into the ongoing need for a better representation of immigrant health professionals. For example, a group of Latino health care advocates in Georgia has encouraged the state's officials

 IP
Primary language and preferred language are often used interchangeably in health care settings. However, a patient's primary language is not necessarily the language he or she prefers to use in communicating with providers. Organizations should inquire about both a patient's primary language and preferred language to determine if there is any distinction in the eyes of the patient.

to adopt a new licensing process for health care providers that would help alleviate the shortage of bilingual physicians and nurses.

Responding to the growing number of immigrants in California—which includes those who need health care as well as professionals in search of meaningful job opportunities—The California Endowment has funded a $1.4 million project to create an International Health Care Workers Assistance Center for the Los Angeles and Southern California area. The first year of the three-year grant included planning, and the center officially opened in 2002.

The purpose of the center is to help physicians, nurses, radiology technicians, respiratory technicians, and others trained in the health field from other countries obtain appropriate licenses and credentials to work in the U.S. health care system. The center will also offer orientation and job placement services. By helping these workers transition to the U.S. health care system, the center will meet the demand for highly trained professionals in communities that desperately need their skills, as well as their linguistic and cultural competency. Additionally, the project addresses the need for racial and ethnic diversity in the health care workforce.[1]

Caldwell Memorial Hospital in Lenoir, North Carolina, recently secured a grant to offer a Spanish language class tailored for its clinical staff through a community college. Case Study 1-1. Gaining Linguistic and Cultural Competence from a Nursing Shortage outlines the ways in which a shortage in nursing staff at the hospital has led to an initiative that addresses cultural and linguistic barriers in the hospital's patient population.

CASE STUDY 1.1
Gaining Linguistic and Cultural Competence from a Nursing Shortage

Caldwell Memorial Hospital is an independent, not-for-profit 110-bed facility serving a rural population of 79,000. It is an acute care hospital with off site physician practices, outpatient services, and a surgery center and wellness center. Its patient population consists of 5% African American, 2.5% Latino, and 92% Caucasian or other.

To avert a shortage in nursing staff, the leaders of Caldwell Memorial reached out to underrepresented persons of its community to draw them into health care careers.

In its county and the five surrounding counties, there are no African American male nurses, 73 African American female nurses, 3 Latino male nurses, and 13 Latino female nurses.

Because adding individuals of diverse backgrounds to its staff represented a shift in its workforce, the hospital anticipated necessary adjustments in its workplace culture. In June of 2003, a specialized, independent company that focuses on diversity training was brought in to conduct an on-site survey of workplace customs. The results of the company's survey led to a personalized three-day training session to train individuals on how to effectively conduct diversity workshops. Since May of last year, Caldwell Memorial has educated more than 500 employees in diversity issues and noticed a positive impact on its patient population and current staff. "This impact will also affect those who will be hired in the future," said Samuel C. Clemmons, R.N., B.S.N., diversity coordinator at the hospital.

With an elevated sense of diversity issues as well as potential linguistic and cultural barriers to care, the hospital has recognized that the services of its 24/7 certified translator service is not enough to keep up with a growing number of Latino patients. Employee surveys are essentially what brought this need to the surface, according to Clemmons. Caldwell Memorial has sought out and secured a grant to cover the costs of a Spanish-language class tailored for its clinical staff through the community college. Through the efforts of newly formed subcommittees, the hospital is also working to have all its forms and hospital signs translated into Spanish.

"In understanding our staff, the public population's culture, and our efforts of bringing underrepresented persons into health care, this awareness training helped us not only prepare for projected staff changes but to better serve our diverse patient population," said Clemmons. "The independent survey was helpful in that it solidified what we knew."

The hospital also requires staff to complete a comprehensive training program that focuses on diversity/cultural competency and is monitored by the hospital's diversity council. Through this training, staff members now better understand and appreciate other cultures and races. "They have also learned how this applies to themselves and their co-workers, those who may look like them but have many differences," said Clemmons.

Clemmons reports that some staff were reluctant to go through this type of training, but those challenges dissipated after the training took hold. "Our then senior V.P. was behind this initiative from the beginning, and now as our CEO/president, she continues to champion this initiative," Clemmons noted. "The only problems were on an individual level, which were cooled due to the way our training is performed." Future activities at the hospital include training specifically geared to managers and supervisors, and additional programming will continue to be considered along with the changing needs of its patient population.

According to Samuel C. Clemmons, R.N., B.S.N., diversity coordinator at Caldwell Memorial Hospital, enhancing the organization's linguistic and cultural competence has involved a team approach. In Clemmons' experience, the elements in Sidebar 1-4. The Essential Elements of Effective Linguistic and Cultural Activities on page 30 ensure the success of linguistic and cultural activities.

What started as a search for new and underrepresented employees has resulted in programming that has reduced complaints and conflicts of both patients and employees in issues involving race or cultural misunderstanding.

Sidebar 1-4.
The Essential Elements of Effective
Linguistic and Cultural Activities

1. You must have a sincere backing of the administration. They first must have a real and proper understanding about all the issues involved in diversity/cultural competency. This is not as clear as it seems.
2. You need a training program that will be received well by the staff.
3. You need a diversity coordinator who is both dedicated and keenly aware of the issues and needs, one who is strong and not shy of "the issues" so he or she will continue to promote diversity in the hospital and in the public. Because many issues will be unpopular, the diversity coordinator must be able to carry on that fight without wavering.
4. You need to find funding to promote or provide training. This can be difficult, and is a reason why many lag behind.

From a business standpoint, Clemmons noted, better patient satisfaction leads to better improvement in your bottom line. When staff is more aware and better able to understand linguistic and cultural differences among its fellow staff members, and those that it serves, a healthy workplace emerges where the costs attributed to changes in staff will be greatly reduced.

Weighing the Financial Costs of Medical Interpretation Services

Ensuring that the entire health care organization is linguistically accessible can be a costly and complex task in large settings with multiple language needs. Studies have suggested that many health care providers do not provide adequate interpreter services because of the financial burden such services impose.[2] These providers, however, should take into account both the consequences of not providing the services and the potential cost benefits of improving communication with their patients.

As mentioned, foundations have played an important role in supporting bilingual training of both providers and staff. One study looking to acquire a better understanding of the costs and benefits of professional interpreter services assessed the impact of implementing a new interpreter service program on the cost and utilization of health care services among patients with limited English proficiency. In the study, conducted from 1991 to 1997 in four health centers of a large Massachusetts HMO, cost data included both the direct costs of providing interpreter services and the costs of net changes in health care utilization that occurred after the new services were implemented.[2]

The study concluded that providing professional interpreter services in a large staff-model HMO increased delivery of health care to LEP patients. The study showed that the majority of the increase in cost of care was attributable to the provision of interpreter services. Patients who used the new interpreter services had significant increases in preventive services, physician visits, and prescription drugs, which suggests that interpretive services enhanced these patients' access to primary and preventive care for a moderate increase in cost.[2] The study's authors consider this cost to be reasonable in the context of reimbursement costs for other types of care during this time period.

Setting the Foundation to Improve Equal Access to Care

The growth of LEP populations and the creation of related legal requirements and guidelines have increased the consciousness of the issue of language access and equal access to quality health care.

Foundations can play a critical leadership role in the pursuit of this goal. The list of action steps designed for foundations, shown in Sidebar 1-5. Action Steps for Foundations Supporting Linguistic and Cultural Competence on page 32, can also be applied to the leaders of health care organizations, community leaders, patient advocates, and policymakers.

Sidebar 1-5. Action Steps for Foundations Supporting Linguistic and Cultural Competence

Foundations can support linguistic and cultural competence in the following ways:
- Promote awareness among providers about the importance of language services and the providers' obligation to make them available. Equip providers with resources, such as medical education and experiential learning opportunities, to enable them to better serve their patients.
- Facilitate agreements among health plans to create an industry standard for covering the costs of professional interpretation services.
- Develop and broadly disseminate high-quality health education materials in multiple languages.
- Tap into resources outside the U.S., such as material already translated in other countries, to strengthen the work done here.
- Increase public awareness of the availability of interpreter services and empower patients with information on what types of questions to ask in the health care encounter.
- Build the field of professional medical interpretation through enhanced educational opportunities, standards development, and recognition of interpreters as integral to the health care team.
- Develop an agenda for long-term sustainable funding and for greater utilization of existing funding, such as federal matching grants for state Medicaid programs.
- Build the business case and encourage the development of new financing mechanisms that could lead to the establishment of standard reimbursement policies.
- Create awareness within communities about the issue of language access and work with community members, policymakers, and government officials to support policies that guarantee equal access to linguistic services.
- Support financial incentives that encourage the use of interpreters, both at the policy level and at the institutional level.
- Help communities explore systems change and policy development to ensure the sustainability of initial investments, including seed money provided for interpreter training and certification.
- Support research to identify and evaluate the most effective modes of delivering the language services in specific communities, including technological advancements.
- Use grants as a mechanism for advancing the field by putting stipulations into awards that grantees must incorporate cultural competence into their projects.
- Work with nontraditional partners, such as anthropologists and arts councils, to better understand how cultural practices influence health.

Source: Grantmakers in Health: In the right words: Addressing language and culture in providing health care. Issue brief no. 18:39–40, 2003. Used with permission.

References

1. Grantmakers in Health: In the right words: Addressing language and culture in providing health care. Issue brief no. 18:5–8, Aug. 2003.

2. Jacobs E.A., et al: Overcoming language barriers in health care: Costs and benefits of interpreter services. *American Journal of Public Health* 94(5):866–869, May 2004.

3. Flores G.: Errors in medical interpretation and their potential clinical consequences in pediatric encounters. *Pediatrics* 111(1):6–14, Jan. 2003.

4. Yeo S.: Language barriers and access to care. *Annual Review of Nursing Research* 22:60–61, 2004.

5. Smedley B.D., Stith A.Y., Nelson A.R. (eds.): *Unequal Treatment: Confronting Racial and Ethnic Disparities in Health Care.* Committee on Understanding and Eliminating Racial and Ethnic Disparities in Health Care. The National Academies Press. National Academy of Sciences, 2003.

6. The Center for Linguistic and Cultural Competence in Health Care: Glossary of terms. *Office of Minority Health Home Page*, U.S. Department of Health and Human Services, Mar. 4, 2003. www.omhrc.gov/cultural/glossary.htm (last accessed May 6, 2005).

7. Yeo S., Fetters M., Maeda Y.: Japanese couples' childbirth experiences in Michigan: Implications for care. *Birth* 27:191–198, 2000.

8. Carey Jackson J., et al: Development of a cervical cancer control intervention program for Cambodian American women. *Journal of Community Health* 25:359–375, 2000.

9. Feinberg E., et al: Language proficiency and the enrollment of Medicaid-eligible children in publicly funded health insurance programs. *Maternal and Child Health Journal* 6(1):5–18, 2002.

10. Schillinger D.: Literacy and language: Disentangling measures of access, utilization, and quality. *JGIM* (19):288–290, Mar. 2004.

11. Mayer G.G., Villaire M.: Health literacy: An ethical responsibility. *Healthcare Executive* p. 50, July/Aug. 2003.

12. Institute of Medicine (IOM) of the National Academies: Health Literacy: A Prescription to End Confusion, Apr. 8, 2004, IOM Home Page. www.iom.edu/report.asp?id=19723 (last accessed May 11, 2005).

13. Andrulis D., Goodman N., Pryor C.: What a Difference an Interpreter Can Make: Health Care Experiences of Uninsured with Limited English Proficiency. Boston: The Access Project, Apr. 2002.

14. Weech-Maldonado R., et al: Racial and ethnic differences in parents' assessments of pediatric care in Medicaid managed care. *Health Services Research* 36(3):575–594, 2001.

15. Ghandi T.K., et al: Drug complications in outpatients. *Journal of General Internal Medicine* 15:149–154, 2000.

16. Hampers L.C., et al: Language barriers and resource utilization in a pediatric emergency department. *Pediatrics* 103(6):1253–1256, 1999.

17. Simmons J.C. (ed.): Putting the spotlight on health literacy to improve quality care. *The Quality Letter for Healthcare Leaders* pp. 2–11, Jul. 2003.

18. Hochhauser M.: Is it ethical to give out unreadable information? *Managed Care Quarterly* pp. 34–36, Spring 2003.

19. Greenbaum M., Flores G.: Lost in translation: Professional interpreters needed to help hospitals treat immigrant patients. *Modern Healthcare* p. 21, May 3, 2004.

20. Kilgannon C.: Queens hospitals learn many ways to say "ah." Immigrant populations with native remedies. *New York Times* p. 21, Apr. 15, 2005.

21. Gravely S.: When your patients speak Spanish—and you don't. *RN* 64(5):65–67, May 2001.

Two

Overcoming
Health Barriers
Through
Cultural Competence

Rapidly changing ethnic demographics in the U.S. and a health care system that is difficult to navigate are forcing health care organizations to come to terms with what cultural competence means and how "competent" they are as health care organizations.[1]

Consider the example of an elderly, first-generation Laotian man who was prescribed four teaspoons a day of an oral antibiotic. Although the gentleman was able to get his prescription filled, when a public health nurse visited his home, she realized he was not taking his medicine because he had no idea what a teaspoon was.[2]

This chapter delves into the concepts of culture and the practices of cultural competence, and considers the effect that misconceptions can have on medical viewpoints. In defining key terms, it also discusses the health disparities linked to cultural barriers between patient and provider. This chapter outlines strategies of cultural assessment, provides a self-assessment tool, and looks at the unique challenges of a hospital that treats one million patients annually; one third of its patients are international.

Understanding the Depth of Diversity in Health Care

In defining and assessing cultural competence, it is important that health care organizations consider what we now understand as "diversity."

In professional literature, diversity is most often used to describe variations in race, ethnicity, socioeconomic environment, culture, language, and dialect relative to "mainstream"

I P
Because individual representation, rather than group numbers, may be most relevant for clinical practice, health care organizations must look at variation in terms of breadth as well as depth of diversity. From this perspective, addressing the issues of diversity is not simply an issue for cities and states with high-density diversity, but is relevant for most parts of the country—even those not commonly thought of as either culturally or linguistically diverse.[1]

standards.[1] In the U.S., mainstream standards are recognized as white, Christian, middle-to-professional class, educated monolingual speakers of General American English (GAE). Because mainstream standards are used as the basis for describing all other groups, exceptions to mainstream standards are seen as different, and have come to be described as "diverse." For example, in this context people who do not speak English as a primary language, African Americans, Muslims, and people living in poverty would be considered diverse. In clinical terms, if a speech language pathologist works with low-income, Spanish-speaking children, she is considered to have a very diverse caseload.[3]

Diversity is often measured in terms of depth—that is, the percentage of people who differ from the "mainstream." But another view of diversity involves its breadth. Breadth of diversity is used to refer to the range or scope of variation within a particular grouping variable, such as language or culture.[1] Clinicians who provide services to several language groups have breadth of variation, regardless of the number of clients within any single language group.

𝒯ERMINOLOGY

Culture is the thoughts, communications, actions, customs, beliefs, values, and institutions of racial, ethnic, religious, or social groups.[4]

Exploring the Concept of Culture in Health Care

Culture is often used as a catch-all term to describe people who are phenotypically similar and have the same beliefs, values, and behaviors. Culture is not race, and cultures are not homogonous or monolithic.[5]

Sidebar 2-1. Defining Culture in Health Care illustrates the ways in which culture relates to health care.

Sidebar 2-1.
Defining Culture in Health Care

Culture defines the following:
- How health care information is received
- How rights and protections are exercised
- What is considered to be a health problem
- How symptoms and concerns about the problem are expressed
- Who should provide treatment for the problem
- What type of treatment should be given
- How beliefs and values—including spiritual, relational, and social—impact understanding, communication, treatment, and compliance.

Source: The Center for Linguistic and Cultural Competence in Health Care: Glossary of Terms. *Office of Minority Health Home Page*, U.S. Department of Health and Human Services, March 4, 2003. www.omhrc.gov/cultural/glossary.htm (last accessed May 6, 2005).

Considering Modifications in Culture

Varying levels of acculturation, assimilation, age, education, income, family structure, gender, wealth, foreign versus U.S.-born status, and refugee or immigrant status all modify the degree to which one's cultural group membership may influence health practices and health status. Each cultural group, such as Cambodian American or African American, is not a monolithic, or static group.[5] In a multicultural society such as the U.S., each cultural

 I P
Inaccurately conceptualizing the term *culture* risks stereotypical thinking, which goes against the grain of scientific research showing that less than 5% of diseases are genetically caused, and that the other 95% are due to lifestyle/environmental factors.[5]

group is steadily undergoing modifications—including mixed marriages—that make it different from the cultural group of origin.

But lifestyle changes are not easy for most patients. Studies on adherence to medical treatments show that only 20%–50% of medical regimens are followed. Patients resist lifestyle changes, and it is culture that forms lifestyle.[5]

The Benefits of Understanding Cultural Differences

Health care itself is a cultural construct that arises from beliefs about the nature of disease and the human body. Cultural issues, therefore, are actually central in the delivery of health services treatment and preventive interventions.

Case Study 2-1. African American Initiative For Male Health Improvement, Henry Ford Health System, Detroit, on pages 40 and 41, looks at the inventive strategy Detroit's Henry Ford Health System undertook in responding to the cultural behaviors of some African American males facing severe illness.

 I P
Organizations, practitioners, and others must understand, value, and incorporate the cultural differences of America's diverse population—as well as examine their own health-related values and beliefs—to support a health care system that responds appropriately to and directly serves the unique needs of populations whose cultures may be different from the prevailing culture.[4]

CASE STUDY 2.1
African American Initiative For Male Health Improvement, Henry Ford Health System, Detroit

Kimberlydawn Wisdom, M.D., now surgeon general of Michigan, was a senior staff physician and researcher in the Department of Emergency Medicine at Henry Ford Health System, Detroit. For too long she had watched African American men come into the emergency department with severe illness, many times the result of diabetes. She often found that even if they knew they had the disease, the men were unaware of how to manage it. One of her patients told an interviewer, "We'll be macho and half dead before we do something about it. If there are 10 men in a room and you ask the black ones about what kind of health issues they have, 90% of them will say, 'Ask my doctor; he knows.' The white men will know what is wrong with them."

Wisdom, in researching the situation, found that African American male diabetics usually present for care later in the course of the disease. Their diabetes is also often complicated by hypertension, which is, unfortunately, commonplace among these patients. Furthermore, she said, these men may be unwilling to admit that they are ill because it implies weakness.

In 1999, supported by grants from her organization and other sources, Wisdom launched the African American Initiative for Male Health Improvement (AIMHI). Using a van and visiting places in southeastern Michigan where health care access is compromised, she and her colleagues offered screening for and education about diabetes, cholesterol, hypertension, and eye conditions. They went to locations ranging from community centers to barbershops. The van continues to visit 60 sites a year.

An AIMHI clinic is now in Detroit. It accepts men, women, and children; Wisdom says that 50% of the clinic's patients are women who have accompanied men to the center. In the past three years, AIMHI has been able to screen more than 7,000 people; at least a third tested positive for either diabetes or hypertension.

Wisdom explained, "For the African American man to reach healthy middle age, he must overcome three major obstacles: infant mortality, adolescent crises, and premature death as a result of chronic disease. We are hoping that through our work, we can see to it that those men who have overcome the first two obstacles can do the same with the third."

Henry Ford Health System recently launched the Institute on Multicultural Health. Sidebar 2-2. Setting Goals in Cultural Competence, on page 41, presents the Institute on Multicultural Health's four goals.

Sidebar 2-2.
Setting Goals in Cultural Competence

1. Conduct research on improving health outcomes for people of color
2. Eliminate racial and ethnic disparities in health status
3. Provide culturally competent care in both research and clinical settings
4. Provide community-based outreach to underserved populations[6]

Reprinted from *Hospitals & Health Networks*, by permission, August 2003. Copyright 2003, by Health Forum, Inc.

Defining Cultural Competence and Recognizing Disparities

The ideas and methods of cultural competence continue to emerge throughout the health care industry. The concepts and uses of terms such as diversity, mainstream, and culture are becoming more common. This is an encouraging sign that those who experience barriers to health care are becoming a priority to those who provide health care.

The federal government defines culturally and linguistically appropriate services (CLAS) as "health care services that are respectful of and responsive to cultural and linguistic needs." Sidebar 2-3. Variations in Culture offers a list of cultural variations.

Sidebar 2-3. Variations in Culture

Cultural competency is based on the concept that cultural differences extend beyond race and ethnicity. Cultural variations include the following:

- Race
- Country of origin
- Native language
- Social class
- Religion
- Mental or physical abilities
- Heritage
- Acculturation
- Age
- Gender
- Sexual orientation
- Other characteristics that may result in a different perspective or decision-making process

Source: Health Resources and Services Administration, U.S. Department of Health and Human Services: Bridging cultures and enhancing care: Approaches to cultural and linguistic competency in managed care. *Health Resources and Services Administration Home Page*, May 30, 2002. www.hrsa.gov/financeMC/bridging-cultures (last accessed May 10, 2005).

Identifying Cultural Disparities in Health Care

Racial and ethnic disparities exist in our health care system. As the previous chapter points out, these disparities are consistent across a range of illnesses and health care services. One out of three U.S. residents today is a member of a racial or ethnic minority group,[1] and because diversity brings challenges in many settings the medical field generally believes that many do not receive equal access to quality care.

Studies of racial and ethnic differences in cardiovascular care provide some of the most convincing evidence of health care disparities. The most thorough studies in this area assess both potential underuse and overuse of services and appropriateness of care by controlling for disease severity using well-established clinical and diagnostic or matched patient controls.[8]

The Effects from Disparities in Ordinary Life

Racial and ethnic disparities are found in many sectors of American life and, unfortunately, some discrimination remains. African Americans, Hispanics, American Indians, and Pacific Islanders, and some Asian American subgroups are disproportionately represented in the lower socioeconomic ranks, in lower quality schools, and in poorer-paying jobs.[8] These disparities can be traced to many factors, including historic patterns of legalized segregation and discrimination. Much of American social and economic life remains ordered by race and ethnicity, with minorities disadvantaged relative to whites.

Many studies suggest that minorities' experiences in the world outside the health care practitioner's office are likely to affect their perceptions and responses in care settings. For example, some studies have shown that minority patients are more likely to refuse recommended services,[9] adhere poorly to treatment regimens,[10] and delay seeking care.[11] These behaviors and attitudes can develop as a result of a poor cultural match between minority patients and their providers, mistrust and misunderstanding of provider instructions, poor prior interactions with health care systems, or simply from a lack of knowledge of how to best use health care services.[8]

In fact, all ethnic minority populations in the U.S. lag behind European Americans (whites) on almost every health indicator, including health care coverage, access to care, and life expectancy, while surpassing whites in almost all acute and chronic disease rates.[12]

Examining the Effects of Cultural Characteristics on Medical Viewpoints

Patients who experience health care disparities often feel they have difficulty communicating with their physicians, and believe they would receive better care if they were of a different race or ethnicity. Through culturally competent interactions that promote the delivery of timely and effective clinical services to patients of diverse backgrounds, health care providers can make an impact in improving health care experiences for minority patients.

The ways in which an individual's culture can affect his or her viewpoint of medical care go beyond the ability to understand, manage, and cope with illness. They can include the following:

- The meaning of a diagnosis
- The compliance and consequences of medical treatment
- The expectation of reporting symptoms
- How much information is desired
- How death and dying will be managed
- Bereavement patterns
- Gender roles
- Family participation
- Decision making[13]

Another issue for health care professionals to consider is patient use of complementary treatments from their unique cultural or spiritual tradition. For example, among certain Native Americans the ritual of peyote is used to "find one's soul" as a treatment to particular illnesses. Patient noncompliance is often grounded in religious beliefs such as the patient's understanding of the result of divine punishment, the value of suffering, or view of a divine plan.

The values and beliefs of patients also impact their communication on numerous health-related issues. Culturally held attitudes affect how patients identify a medical problem requiring professional attention versus self- or home-care. Patients may perceive certain topics as

 I P
The beliefs and values of individual patients—and the ways these beliefs and values impact their view of certain medical treatment or procedures—is of significant importance, and must be respected by the health care team and incorporated into treatment rather than minimized or rejected. The Joint Commission holds organizations accountable for addressing and maintaining patient rights, including "respecting and acknowledging one's psychosocial, spiritual, and cultural values and how they impact a patient's response to his or her care."

taboo and feel uncomfortable discussing them, especially if the provider is of the opposite sex or from a different religious or cultural tradition. Describing such a problem to the provider can be challenging for patients. If patients disagree with the provider, cultural attitudes may inhibit them from sharing their concerns.

Conflicting Beliefs Between Patients and Providers

Each clinician develops his or her own lens to view reality, which is typically influenced by the clinician's native culture and modified by professional socialization and his or her exposure to Western biomedicine. These sets of beliefs and values converge to varying

T I P
To develop effective approaches to clinical communication, health care professionals must be aware that their own worldview may be in conflict with that of a patient's.

degrees to form the clinician's blended worldview. This worldview, however, may conflict with those of the patient or the patient's family. Attitudes and behaviors that are considered the "right" way, or even "mainstream," are dependent on one's worldview.

For example, the cultural edict against telling a Muslim patient that he or she has a terminal diagnosis, which from the Western concept of patient autonomy would be done to foster anticipatory grief counseling, is antithetical to that Western concept. Yet within the context of the cultural belief of some Muslim traditions, to do so would be unethical. In this case, even though grief, bereavement, and mourning are universal responses to dying and to the loss of loved ones, a cultural distinction exists in the ways in which these events are discussed and observed.

In Western medicine, the concept that an individual determines his or her own health is generally accepted; this supports the preventive medicine approach and low-power distance between patients and providers with a Western medicine mind-set. In some cultures, the patient's role is passive and families are viewed as the receivers of information and the decision makers.

Patients from other backgrounds may view things quite differently. They may perceive health and illness as a matter of fate, focusing more on the present state of health rather than the future. Frequently, they may believe the physician has the greater power in the relationship and therefore avoid asking questions about their own condition. Depending on their particular culture and past experiences, as Sidebar 2-4. Unique Patient

---

Sidebar 2-4.
Unique Patient Perceptions of Physicians

- Healer/Miracle worker
- Expert
- God's worker
- Shaman
- Confidant or friend of the family
- Authority figure or recipient of unquestioned respect
- Pill dispenser
- Last resort for healing
- Someone who inflicts pain
- Partner in making health decisions

Source: Health Resources and Services Administration, U.S. Department of Health and Human Services: Bridging cultures and enhancing care: Approaches to cultural and linguistic competency in managed care. *Health Resources and Services Administration Home Page*, May 30, 2002. www.hrsa.gov/financeMC/bridging-cultures (last accessed May 10, 2005).

Perceptions of Physicians indicates, patients from minority backgrounds may perceive a physician in unique ways.

Like every provider, each patient possesses his or her own beliefs and behaviors. However, some common characteristics have been associated with particular immigrant populations. Sidebar 2-5. Common Characteristics Associated with Immigrant Populations, on pages 46 and 47, outlines these common characteristics.

The emerging prominent role of clinically trained, professional board-certified chaplains working with health care organizations in completing spiritual assessments, functioning as the "cultural broker," and leading cultural and spiritual sensitivity assessments for staff and physicians can be of great value.

---

*T*ERMINOLOGY

Spirituality refers to an inner belief system. It is a delicate "spirit-to-spirit" relationship to oneself and others, and the God of one's understanding.[12]

Religion refers to the externals of one's belief system: church, prayers, traditions, rites, and rituals, among others.[12]

Spiritual needs can be identified in a variety of ways. Visual clues and symbols include the Bible, Torah, Koran, Book of Mormon, prayer beads, rosaries, and a cross among others. Prayer, meditation, grace before meals, and singing are among the behaviors that signal a patient's spiritual practice, as is talking about God, faith, and prayer.[12]

The professional chaplain on staff can assist the interdisciplinary team in understanding cultural, spiritual, and religious issues that emerge and how they can be integrated into the patients' plan of care. Most people consider themselves to be spiritual beings, not everyone is religious.

Understanding the Challenges that Differences Create

Understanding patients' family issues promotes more culturally competent care. The family structure and make-up, such as who lives in the household and who are the decision makers, can be important when treating patients. A patient's preferred language may be different than that of other family members, and the extent of acculturation may differ as well. Again, a patient's preferred language may also differ from his or her primary language.

Providers must understand each individual rather than making assumptions about one family member based on familiarity with another. Internal family conflict can impact the care process. Organizations should be aware that signs of conflict could in some cases help guide providers as they treat multiple members of the same family.

> *T* I P
> Being sensitive to spiritual issues and including spiritual prayer is an essential component of providing quality care and support for patients and their families.[12]

Sidebar 2-5.
Common Characteristics
Associated with Immigrant Populations

Many Hispanics tend to see illness as the result of an imbalance in the body, so emphasis is placed on maintaining good health through a balance of eating, working, and praying. The mother tends to determine when a family member requires medical care, and the male head of the household gives permission to go to the health care facility.

The Hispanic patient may believe that God determines the outcome of his or her illness and that he or she is the victim and is expected to be passive. In many cases, the family would prefer to hear about bad medical news before the patient. A family spokesperson may wish to communicate with the patient about the severity of the illness.

The African American culture, among others, comprises various ethnic subgroups that differ from one another. Differences also can exist based on age, education, and place of birth. For example, an African American may perceive his or her illness based on ideas found in the traditional West African culture where illness is often perceived as a lack of harmony or conflict in an individual's life.

The African American experience in the United States has left many mistrustful of mainstream institutions and providers who are white. To many, the bad faith and abuses of the Tuskegee Syphilis Study are not isolated incidents in history but an example of experiences African Americans endure in health settings.

Religion, spirituality, and kinship may also play an important role in the African American patient's understanding and treatment of illness. Many African Americans place high importance on family and church. It may also take a long time for African American patients to seek health care, preferring self-treatment and giving God a chance to heal the ailment. In addition, extended kinship bonds may exist with grandparents, aunts, uncles, cousins, and with individuals not biologically related, such as trusted friends.

Muslims believe in life after death, and are prohibited from supporting any form of euthanasia or any attempt to shorten life. Those who are ill are exempt from their requirement to fast during the holy month of Ramadan, but they may have special dietary requirements including being forbidden to eat any food upon which any other name has been invoked besides God. Muslim patients may require prayer mats as Friday is a holy day when Muslims pray together. The confession of sins and begging forgiveness must occur in the presence of family before death and, as the moment of death approaches, the Islamic Creed should be recited. Some Muslim customs prohibit handshakes or any contact between genders and only female health care staff should care for Muslim girls

(continued)

Sidebar 2-5. *(continued)*

and women when possible. Muslim women might also request wearing gowns that observe clothing restrictions.[12]

Asian/Pacific Islanders can be significantly influenced by the extended family. The oldest male is often the decision maker and spokesperson. In many cases, the interest and honor of the family are more important than those of the individual. Respect and harmony are two cultural themes within this group. Older family members are respected and their opinions are often unquestioned—conflict is avoided, particularly disagreements with health care professionals. However, just because the family does not raise objections with the health care provider does not mean the treatment regimen will be followed.

Source: Joint Commission Resources: *Improving the Care Experience.* Oakbrook Terrace, IL: Joint Commission Resources, 2000.

Assessing Levels of Cultural Embeddedness

An important aspect of an organization's educational assessment process is to determine how embedded the patient is in his or her traditional culture.

The extent to which a patient is influenced by his or her culture has a major influence on his or her approach to patient education. A patient who still has close ties with his or her original culture may not have as much contact with the country's predominant culture and, therefore, with the terms and processes of Western medical care. Whether the patient has recently immigrated to the United States and whether that immigration was voluntary may have significant impact on the patient's perspective. Questions that can help determine cultural embeddedness include the following:

- How recently did the patient immigrate? Was it voluntary or involuntary?
- What country did the patient emigrate from and how different is that culture from U.S. culture?
- Does the patient wear clothing representative of the country from which they emigrated? Follow traditional dietary habits?
- Does the patient leave his or her neighborhood to participate in the larger culture?
- Does the patient use folk medicine or the practices of a native healer?[14]

I P
No one definitive curriculum on culturally competent communication exists, but those providers who make attempts to learn about and understand the cultural backgrounds of their particular community of patients are best equipped to engage in effective culturally competent communications.

*𝒯*ERMINOLOGY

Cultural embeddedness is how aligned a patient is with his or her native culture.[14]

Addressing Alternative Health Practices and a Lack of Trust in Diverse Populations

Patients, regardless of background, are more frequently turning to alternative therapies. Acupuncture and other traditional therapies are proving to be effective treatments, and the spiritual and mental aspects of disease are receiving more attention now than ever.

Complementary medicine and alternative health practices are common approaches to maintaining wellness and treating illness among patients of diverse backgrounds. One in three people has used these methods; however, nearly two-thirds do not tell their regular physician about the use of complementary medicine.[14] This is a major concern because of potential treatment interactions. In some cultures, patients may view Western medicine as a last resort because they feel it is too potent.

Building Trust to Strengthen Patient Assessments

Perhaps most important in patient assessment and interaction is to establish a level of trust with patients. When trust is absent from both the patient and provider perspective, health care disparity can occur.

*𝒯***I P**

Assessing the cultural embeddedness of patients can help providers determine effective approaches to patient education.

Physicians have limited time to spend with patients, and patients may perceive that physicians are driven by profits even if this is not actually the case. A basic lack of trust between patients and providers results in a lack of trust in the diagnosis or treatment of the medical problem. Patients may feel they need to do their own research to validate treatment recommendations and be more proactive and aggressive to get quality care.

Conducting a Self-Assessment of Cultural Competence

In most cases, cultural insensitivity is not intentional. We have a natural tendency to assume that our own beliefs, customs, and values are the most sensible. The first step in becoming more culturally sensitive, then, is for us to become aware of the cultural assumptions from which we develop our judgments.[12]

Each and every health care professional plays a role in improving cultural competence. Clinicians who assess their own cultural competence can gain insight into how a change in their individual perspectives can lead to improvements in organizational care. The self-assessment tool in Sidebar 2-6. Conducting a Cultural Competence Self-Assessment, on pages 49–51, is one construct designed to gauge individual perspectives in cultural competence.

Sidebar 2-6.
Conducting a Cultural Competence Self-Assessment

Directions: Enter A, B, or C for each item listed below.
These letters represent the following:

A. Things I do frequently
B. Things I do occasionally
C. Things I do rarely or never

Physical Environment, Materials, and Resources

1. _____ I display pictures, posters, artwork, and other décor that reflect the cultures and ethnic backgrounds of clients my program or agency serves.

2. _____ I ensure that magazines, brochures, and other printed material in the reception area are of interest to and reflect the different cultures of individuals and families my practice, program, or agency serves.

3. _____ When using videos, films, or other media resources for health education, treatment, or other interventions, I ensure that they reflect the cultures and ethnic background of individuals and families my practice, program, or agency serves.

4. _____ I ensure that printed information my practice, agency, or program disseminates takes into account the average literacy levels of individuals and families receiving services.

Communication Styles

5. When interacting with individuals and families who have limited English proficiency (LEP), I always keep in mind that:

_____ Limitations in English proficiency are in no way a reflection of their level of intellectual functioning.

_____ Their limited ability to speak the language of the dominant culture has no bearing on their ability to communicate effectively in their language of origin.

_____ They may or may not be literate in their language of origin or English.

6. _____ I use bilingual-bicultural staff and personnel and volunteers skilled or certified in the provision of medical interpretation during treatment, interventions, meetings, or other events for individuals and families who need or prefer this skill or assistance.

7. _____ For individuals and families who speak languages or dialects other than English, I attempt to learn and use key words in their language so I am better able to communicate with them during assessment, treatment, or other interventions.

8. _____ I attempt to determine any familial colloquialisms used by individuals or families that may impact assessment, treatment, or other interventions.

(continued)

Sidebar 2-6. *(continued)*

9. _____ When possible, I ensure that all notices and communiqués to individuals and families are written in their language of origin.

10. _____ I understand that it may be necessary to use alternatives to written communications for some individuals and families, as word of mouth may be a preferred method of receiving information.

Values and Attitudes

11. _____ I avoid imposing values that may conflict with or be inconsistent with those of cultures or ethnic groups other than my own.

12. _____ I screen books, movies, and other media resources for negative cultural, ethnic, or racial stereotypes before sharing them with individuals and families my practice, program, or agency serves.

13. _____ I intervene in an appropriate manner when I observe other staff or clients within my practice, program, or agency engaging in behaviors that show cultural insensitivity, racial biases, and prejudice.

14. _____ I recognize and accept that individuals from culturally diverse backgrounds may desire varying degrees of acculturation into the dominant culture.

15. _____ I understand and accept that family (including extended family members and godparents, among others) is defined differently by different cultures.

16. _____ I accept and respect that male-female roles (including who makes major decisions for the family) may vary significantly among different cultures and ethnic groups.

17. _____ I understand that age and life-cycle factors must be considered in interactions with individuals and families. For example, some may place a high value on the decision of elders, on the role of the eldest male or female in the family, or on the roles and expectations of children within the family.

18. _____ Even though my professional or moral viewpoints may differ, I accept individuals and families as the ultimate decision makers for services and supports impacting their lives.

19. _____ I recognize that the meaning or value of medical treatment and health education may vary greatly among cultures.

20. _____ I accept that religion and other beliefs may influence how individuals and families respond to illnesses, disease, and death.

21. _____ I understand that the perception of health, wellness, and preventive health services has different meanings to different cultural or ethnic groups.

22. _____ I recognize and accept that folk and religious beliefs may influence an individual's or family's reaction and approach to a child born with a disability, or later diagnosed with a disability, genetic disorder, or special health care needs.

(continued)

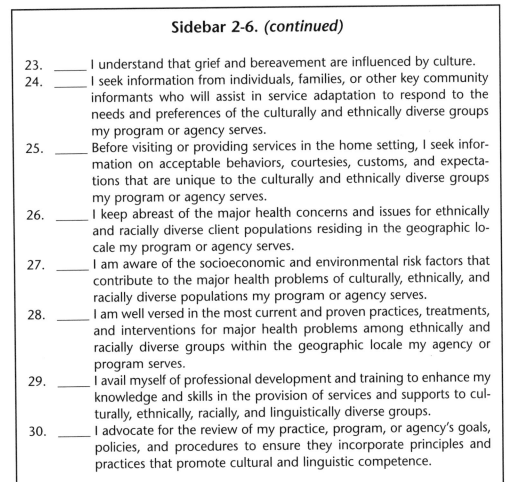

Sidebar 2-6. *(continued)*

23. _____ I understand that grief and bereavement are influenced by culture.
24. _____ I seek information from individuals, families, or other key community informants who will assist in service adaptation to respond to the needs and preferences of the culturally and ethnically diverse groups my program or agency serves.
25. _____ Before visiting or providing services in the home setting, I seek information on acceptable behaviors, courtesies, customs, and expectations that are unique to the culturally and ethnically diverse groups my program or agency serves.
26. _____ I keep abreast of the major health concerns and issues for ethnically and racially diverse client populations residing in the geographic locale my program or agency serves.
27. _____ I am aware of the socioeconomic and environmental risk factors that contribute to the major health problems of culturally, ethnically, and racially diverse populations my program or agency serves.
28. _____ I am well versed in the most current and proven practices, treatments, and interventions for major health problems among ethnically and racially diverse groups within the geographic locale my agency or program serves.
29. _____ I avail myself of professional development and training to enhance my knowledge and skills in the provision of services and supports to culturally, ethnically, racially, and linguistically diverse groups.
30. _____ I advocate for the review of my practice, program, or agency's goals, policies, and procedures to ensure they incorporate principles and practices that promote cultural and linguistic competence.

This checklist is intended to heighten the awareness and sensitivity of personnel to the importance of cultural and linguistic competence in health and human service settings. It provides concrete examples of the kinds of beliefs, attitudes, values, and practices that foster cultural and linguistic competence at the individual or practitioner level. This checklist has no answer key with correct responses. However, if you frequently responded "C," you may not necessarily demonstrate beliefs, attitudes, values, and practices that promote cultural and linguistic competence within health care delivery programs.

Source: Goode TD: "Self-Assessment checklist for personnel providing primary health care services," from *Promoting Cultural Competence and Cultural Diversity for Personnel Providing Services and Supports to Children with Special Health Care Needs and Their Families.* Georgetown University Child Development Center (revised 2004). Used with permission.

I P

In assessing and interacting with patients of diverse backgrounds, staff may observe tension between older family members and younger, more acculturated children. The children may wish to incorporate Western medical practices into treatment while the older, more traditional family members may wish to follow the remedies specific to their culture. Staff should not become involved in these struggles but should respect the two positions and identify opportunities for teaching that recognize both points of view.[14]

Strategies to Improve Cultural Assessment and Interaction

A culturally based systems approach to cultural assessment and interaction requires the practitioner to first be aware of his or her own cultural beliefs and values to recognize when they may differ from those of the patient, and evaluate the patient's responses objectively. Both parties bring their cultural views to the interaction.

As discussed, when the staff member and patient are from different cultural backgrounds, the staff member needs to ask questions that respectfully acknowledge these differences and build the trust necessary for the patient to confide in him or her.[4] One way to begin this dialogue is by conducting a RISK reduction assessment to elicit information about the patient's Resources, Identity, Skills, and Knowledge. This assessment tool appears on page 53 in Table 2-1. "RISK" Risk Reduction Assessments to Ascertain Level of Cultural Influence. Identifying the patient's perspective may help avoid the pitfalls of stereotyping or ignoring the potential influence of culture, and may reduce the risk of miscommunication.

The basic premise of cultural assessment is that patients have a right to their cultural beliefs, values, and practices and that these factors should be understood, respected, and considered when designing and giving culturally competent care and education.[14] This premise includes being sensitive toward diverse groups and being aware of issues regarding culture, race, gender, and sexual orientation.

I P
Providers must strive to establish a connection with patients that will help patients share their feelings and calm their fears.

When assessing a patient's and family's need for health care education, health care workers need to glean culturally related information that can affect the patient's treatment and be sensitive to the cultural differences that exist between the patient and the interviewer. A patient's personal understanding of his or her disease is in many ways more important than the health care professional's view.[14]

Sidebar 2-7. Cultural Awareness Tool in Patient Education on page 54 serves as a guide to approaching patients with a strategy of cultural openness.

Table 2-1. RISK Reduction Assessments to Ascertain Level of Cultural Influence

	Relevant Information	Questions and Strategies
Resources for patients and families	Tangible resources that the family can draw on, such as: level of education, socioeconomic status (including insurance), social support networks, in-language social service agencies, transportation, grocery shopping, etc.	"What kind of assistance is available to you in your community that might be helpful during this time?" "Do you know others in your community who have faced similar difficulties?"
Individual identity and acculturation/assimilation	Questions about the patient, the context of his or her life, and individual circumstances, including place of birth, refugee or immigration status, languages spoken, and degree of integration within the ethnic community.	"Where were you born and raised?" "When did you emigrate to the U.S. and how has your experience been coming to a new country?" "What languages do you speak and in which are you most comfortable talking?" "What are your most important concerns now that you have this illness?" *Life history assessment:* "What were other important times in your life and how might these experiences help us to know you?"
Skills available to the patient and family to adapt to the disease requirements	The actual ability of the family to navigate the health care system and cope with the demands of the disease itself—emotionally, physically, socially, and spiritually.	"Who are the people in your support system that are helpful or harmful?" "Who is there to help you with physical care, emotional support, transportation, and care of loved ones?" "Who do you see or talk with; where do you go for religious or spiritual strength, or solace?"
Knowledge about the ethnic group's health beliefs, values, practices, and cultural etiquette	Beliefs, values and practices associated with communication etiquette and health, including attitudes toward truth-telling, family-centered vs. individual-centered decision-making style, historical, social, and political issues that might affect relationships between the patient and elements of the dominant culture.	The clinician knows the dominant ethnic groups in his or her practice. Reads about the different cultures. Attends continuing education programs about each culture—the beliefs, values, and communication practices surrounding health, including truth-telling. What is the symbolic meaning of the disease? Learns about the usual community and family practices surrounding death and dying; Does the patient/family adhere to any of these beliefs and practices? How are decisions made in this cultural group? Who is the head of the household? Does this family adhere to traditional cultural guidelines or do they adhere more to the Western model?

Source: Kagawa-Singer M., Kassim-Lakha S.: A strategy to reduce cross-cultural miscommunication and increase the likelihood of improving health outcomes. *Academic Medicine* 78(6):583, Jun. 2003. Used with permission.

Sidebar 2-7.
Cultural Awareness Tool in Patient Education

Questions to be considered when conducting a patient interview include:

1. What is your primary name, language, and cultural group?
2. Please describe what your current illness or surgery means to you?
3. Can you tell me about any special things or processes (such as folk medicines or healing remedies) that you use as a form of relaxation or medication?
4. Who in or outside your family helps you make decisions about your illness or surgery?
5. Can and will you share your spiritual beliefs including their influence (if any) on the current illness or surgery?
6. What methods or tools can I, as your health care provider, use to help you learn more about your current illness or surgery?

In the context of providing targeted and appropriate education, health care providers should discover the following about a patient:

- Values
- Meaning of his or her illness
- Language barriers and literacy
- Cultural myths and taboos
- Folk beliefs
- Alternative medical practices
- Spirituality
- Immigration status and country of origin
- Education level
- Relationships with others (such as family or friends)
- Socioeconomic status

Suggestions for working with patients from different cultures include the following:

- Pay close attention to body language—facial expression or lack of response may indicate a conflict
- Ask open-ended questions to gain more information about assumptions and expectations
- Remain nonjudgmental when information given is different from expected [response]
- Take communication cues from the patient regarding touch, eye contact, and so on[*]

Source: Garrity J.: Cultural competence in patient education. *CARING Magazine* 32(8): 18–20, Mar. 2000.

[*]Reprinted with limited permission from the National Association for Home Care & Hospice. All rights reserved.

Promoting Cultural Competence Through Organizational Change

The leaders of health care organizations are equipped and positioned to guide their workforce through the processes of improved care and services. It is they who provide the impetus, set the goals and priorities, support the policies and decisions, and respond to the challenges of positive change.[7] With focused leadership, policies that impact numerous patients can be defined and implemented throughout the organization.

---

*T*ERMINOLOGY
Care means that patients and their families are treated as human beings that have lives beyond the hospital and meaning beyond the medical world of diagnoses, medications, treatment, and prognosis.[12]

Accepting Assumptions in Promoting Cultural Competence

When outlining a strategic approach to promoting cultural competency, an organization's leaders must be willing to accept the following assumptions:

- First, organizations do not change easily. They are made up of multiple staffs, departments, and units. Their functions and operational customs can be very entrenched.
- Second, large change is built on small steps. Again, the size, scope, and processes of health care organizations limit the speed at which new programs, measures, activities, and techniques can be applied.
- Third, even failed attempts at change can be positive, negative, or both, depending on what an organization chooses to learn from the attempts.[7]

With an understanding of these concepts in place, the first step to promoting cultural competency in a large group is to assess the status quo and actual practice.

Initiating Readiness for Change

Another component of strategically promoting cultural competence is increasing readiness for change. Increasing readiness begins by building internal support for the initiative.

With the support of decision makers, a momentum toward the acceptance of change can be forged and agents of change can be mobilized. Increasing and improving cultural competence does not happen overnight. It is important that the expectations of staff are well managed. Setting expectations too high and too fast can result in negative backlash.

*T*IP
Health care providers should approach the patient interview from the position of mutual understanding and collaboration rather than from the position of imposing traditional Western medical practices.

I P
Improving cultural competence often involves initiating significant organizational change. Promoting and improving cultural competence in an organization requires a strategic approach, a solid infrastructure, recognition of the importance of relationship-building, and management knowledge that is essential to other aspects of institutional change.

Credibility and external support are also important in promoting cultural competence and initiating readiness for change. Credibility is gained when decision makers are actively involved in the process and committed to the same culturally appropriate behaviors they are asking of others in the organization.[7] By engaging and encouraging outside agencies to contribute to their efforts—while understanding their motivations to be involved—an organization strengthens its ability to implement change.

Creating a Sustainable Structure for Cultural Competence

After organizational change takes hold, sustaining it and improving upon it depends on a solid infrastructure. When building an infrastructure to sustain the cultural competence development process, organizations should concentrate on the five key elements:

1. Knowledge
2. Planning committee
   (must be ongoing and active)
3. Point person
4. Data
5. Resources[7]

 I P
Organizations should perform assessments to define the context and environment, identify assets and obstacles, and determine readiness to meet patient and community needs. By performing assessments, organizations send a message to staff and the community they serve of the intent to promote cultural competence. Through assessments, they set a baseline for measuring progress in the future.[7]

As with any large-scale project, identifying objectives and goals with actions and timelines will keep the effort on track, and clearly identifying current and future resources will assess the sustainability of the efforts.

Financial resources are an important part of cultural competency improvement and sustainability, but human resources are just as valuable. Members at all levels of the organization need to believe that these efforts are authentic, will promote better delivery of health care services, and are critical to the overall success of the group.

Routinely communicating the strategic plan and its development to the entire organization

I P
With strong leadership that
works to gain both internal
and external support for its
efforts, an organization lays the
groundwork and initiates the
readiness for change.

will strengthen the process, limit internal
conflicts,[7] and help ensure its sustainability.

Other strategies have been forwarded to
help health care organizations promote and
enhance cultural competence and, ultimately,
improve patient safety. Sidebar 2-8. Strategies
to Enhance Cultural Competence on pages 58
and 59 includes examples of leadership, communication, care provision, and educational
strategies.

Case Study 2-2. A Unique Hospital Overcomes Unique Challenges Through
Improvements in Linguistic and Cultural Competence on pages 59–62 spotlights an
international health care organization with such a diverse patient population that virtually
every aspect of its operation depends on linguistic and cultural competence.

I P
Praise and recognition are often the strongest ways to gain internal support.
Acknowledging those individuals who are unwavering in embracing change
encourages others to follow.

Sidebar 2-8.
Strategies to Enhance Cultural Competence

Leadership Strategies

Devote resources to cultural training and education efforts and integrate initiatives into all levels of the organization. Cultural training cannot be a one-time event; it must be an ongoing process. Leaders must commit the needed resources, including people, time, and dollars.

Assess the cultural composition of the staff and make diversity a priority in hiring practices. Staff members who practice or are familiar with the values, beliefs, traditions, customs, and cultures present in the organization's service area can be recruited through development of relationships with cultural groups in the area.

Communication Strategies

Use appropriately trained medical interpreters and translators. Untrained or poorly trained interpreters can make translation errors that could jeopardize patient safety.

Use ad hoc translators with extreme caution. Using visitors in the waiting room, nonclinical staff members who just happen to speak the patient's language, and children and other family members should be avoided, if at all possible. These individuals are not knowledgeable about patient confidentiality, medical terminology, and informed consent. Confidentiality and safety breaches could result. Family members may also withhold information during the translation process or intentionally change the meaning to protect the patient.

Listen carefully and respectfully to beliefs about illnesses and traditional cures. A patient's beliefs about the causes of illness will affect his or her future behavior. Practitioners need to hear, understand, and explore such beliefs to develop treatment programs that are likely to be followed by the patient.

Use professionals who possess the training and competence to assist. For example, board-certified chaplains are valuable resources in identifying and communicating patient/family beliefs that need to be acknowledged, addressed, and incorporated into the plan of care.

Care Provision Strategies

Clarify patient and family instructions through demonstration and visual aids. Whether language is a barrier—and particularly if it is a barrier—patients understand instructions better, and hence can comply better, when they see staff members demonstrate what they need to do. To ensure the patient understands the instructions, staff members can request a return demonstration.

(continued)

Sidebar 2-8. *(continued)*

Do not stereotype people. Educational materials, such as "culture tools" that provide snapshot information about belief practices, nutritional preferences, communication issues, and other matters, can be used as a starting point to understand and identify appropriate cultural issues and common practices of populations. However, staff cannot assume that the descriptions of cultural groups appearing on such tools apply to every individual in the group.

For example, one tool may note that Koreans are reserved with strangers and Jamaicans are curious and tend to ask a lot of questions. This may generally be true across these populations, but it cannot be assumed for each individual in the group.

Educational Strategies

Integrate cultural sensitivity into orientation and continuing education courses. Courses, such as those on communicating with patients, can include cultural role-playing, and patients can be invited to talk about their health care experiences in the United States, their traditional cures, and cultural values.

Make staff aware of diversity information resources. The Joint Commission provides links to approximately 45 organizations involved in efforts to enhance cultural competence in health care online at http://www.jcaho.org/about+us/hlc/links.htm.

The Office of Minority Health's (OMH) National Standards for Culturally and Linguistically Appropriate Services (CLAS), at http://www.omhrc.gov/CLAS, is another good place to start.

Source: The Impact of Cultural Competence on Patient Safety. *Joint Commission Perspectives on Patient Safety*™ 4(10): 1–9, Oct. 2004.

*C*ASE STUDY 2.2
A Unique Hospital Overcomes
Unique Challenges Through Improvements
in Linguistic and Cultural Competence

Bumrungrad International is a 554-bed hospital located in the heart of Bangkok. The hospital treats more than one million patients annually from more than 150 countries. The hospital is Asia's first Joint Commission International accredited facility and is active in clinical care, teaching, clinical research, and international hospital management.

The hospital treats 2,900 outpatients daily and has an average inpatient census of 350. The hospital operates as a one-stop center for medical care, integrating 33 outpatient clinics, diagnostics, lab, therapeutics, and surgical services, all under one roof. The hospital is recognized as Thailand's premier medical center and a regional referral center for advanced care. Bumrungrad International has more than 600 Thai physicians (200 of which are U.S. board certified) and 800 nurses.

Unique Hospital, Unique Challenges

Of the one million patients it treats annually, more than 350,000 (or one third) are international patients, making Bumrungrad International the world's largest provider of medical services to a nonlocal or foreign population. The hospital is a pioneer in medical tourism, attracting patients from all over the world for medical services ranging from annual checkups to plastic surgery to cancer treatment.

The hospital's success internationally poses a significant challenge in the form of communication and adapting to cultures that often collide with Thai culture and sensitivities. Case in point: The hospital treated 4,000 Arabic-speaking patients in year 2000. In 2004, Bumrungrad treated more than 50,000 Arabic-speaking patients. The exponential rise in this patient population created a significant culture shock for the Thai staff as it tried to service these patients, who come from a culture vastly different from the staff's own.

As will be discussed later, the hospital addresses these challenges organizationwide and requires each department to develop specific action plans to manage the situation. Such activities and programs are a team effort directed by senior management.

Identifying the Need for Cultural and Linguistic Improvement

While Bumrungrad operates in predominantly two languages—Thai and English—the hospital staff has had to become proficient in other languages, such as Japanese, Chinese, and Arabic, because these languages represent some 35% of Bumrungrad's total international patient population. Hospital leaders recognized very early on that the hospital's success in attracting and treating international patients directly correlated to its ability to communicate and adapt to its patients.

Addressing Cultural and Linguistic Competence

First, the hospital identified foreign language competency and communication as a critical issue in its business plan. By doing so, leaders made it a priority for all departments—medical and nonmedical—and required each department to incorporate specific action items to address this issue. Second, the organization focused more resources on the problem. This included hiring more foreign language staff, engaging staff in language and cultural education training, and producing more foreign language materials such as patient instruction material, brochures, and signage. Finally, Bumrungrad International made changes to its facilities and services to accommodate patient's needs, including adding halal-prepared food to its menu and a prayer room for its Muslim and Arabic-speaking patients.

Key Issues that Triggered Improvement Initiatives

The impetus for change at Bumrungrad arose, first and foremost, out of patient safety.

Communication is critical in service industries, and even more so in health care. Other issues included the competitive advantage the organization would gain over its competitors by better understanding and meeting its patients' needs and, of course, patient retention.

In the case of safety issues, the organization's Total Quality Management (TQM) department identified areas where patient safety could be compromised. Customer feedback was also a very valuable tool, as patients expressed what their needs and expectations were so the organization could respond to specific demands. Arabic patients, for example, complained that the facility did not have enough interpreters or medical staff fluent in Arabic. The organization immediately brought on Arabic language staff and a physician medical coordinator fluent in Arabic. Issues relating to patient retention and positioning were addressed primarily by the organization's marketing department.

Taking and Testing Steps Toward Change

In terms of language competency, the organization's human resources department began to test staff for foreign language capabilities and instituted a financial rewards system based on members' level of fluency in one or more foreign languages. In the clinics, Bumrungrad produced simple, easy-to-use booklets with patient instructions in several languages to facilitate communication with patients. This was especially effective in radiology where simple instructions to patients such as "hold your breath" were needed but did not require the services of an interpreter.

Bumrungrad International's customer services department held instructional classes to help staff greet patients in several languages. The hospital also hired more staff who spoke foreign languages and deployed these people in key areas, including registration, clinics, and cashier. Certain elements were tested, such as language proficiency, but success was otherwise gauged on customer feedback.

Implementing the process of change was a cross-departmental effort that took place concurrently within all departments and independently within each department. Bumrungrad's business plan identifies critical success factors that apply to the organization as a whole, and then asks each department to develop specific action items to address this issue. The organization could not afford to wait to roll out these changes item by item, but rather tackled the issue organizationwide. The organization recognized the benefit was speed but the challenge was to ensure follow through and coordination among the various departments.

Measuring the success of the cultural and linguistic competence improvements TQM reports provided the organization with information on incidents relating to miscommunication or manner. Customer feedback also helped the hospital gauge its progress in this area because it was specifically interested in learning if communication and manner complaints were rising or falling. The organization's census, however, proved to be one of the most effective tools of measurement because happy customers come back and refer an organization's services to others. On average, Bumrungrad's international business has grown 25% per year for the past six years.

Overcoming Barriers to Change

Internally, it took several years for Bumrungrad's staff—medical and support—to adjust to the influx of international patients, whose attitudes and behavior sometimes clashed with Thai culture. For example, according to some Thais, Arabs speak loudly and in a manner that Thais perceive as aggressive. This tended to make many of the facility's staff uncomfortable and sometimes unwilling to help. Bumrungrad has also had problems obtaining work visas for the primary language speakers it wants to employ.

Lessons Learned in Instituting Improvement Efforts

First, any organization that wants to improve a particular element of its business should address the issue as part of its business planning process, according to the leaders at Bumrungrad. An organization cannot effectively address a critical issue if it is not integrated within the organization's business plan. Second, change disrupts the status quo and there will always be those who do not understand or approve of the direction an organization is taking. An organization's own people must be won over before it is able to win over its customers. Third, rewards are a great motivator and it is important that staff tangibly sees and feels the benefits of the changes being made.

Carrying on the Improvement Effort

The improvements made at Bumrungrad have helped differentiate it from other hospitals in Thailand and the region. It has gained a competitive advantage. These improvements have resulted in better and safer patient management (quality), and have reinforced its position as the leading international hospital in Asia. Improving communication and cultural education is not a program, according to the hospital's leaders, but rather a process. This process of improving capabilities at Bumrungrad will continue year after year.

Culturally competent health care not only contributes to better health outcomes and more satisfied patients, it can also be cost efficient. It creates an environment in which the provider is able to obtain more specific and complete information, allowing the provider to make a more appropriate diagnosis. It facilitates the development of treatment plans that the patient follows and the family supports. It reduces delays in seeking care and leads to greater use of health services. It enhances overall communication, and improves the clinical interaction between provider and patient. It forges compatibility between Western health practices and traditional cultural health practices.[14]

But, as the next chapter discusses, the positive outcomes from improved linguistic and cultural competence rely on the contributions of those being served. To better serve a specific population, organizations must not only be dedicated to understanding that community, but also be committed to working in partnership with that community.

References

1. Larson L.: Is your hospital culturally competent? And what does that mean exactly? *Trustee* 58(2): 20–23, Feb. 2005.
2. Families USA Foundation: Cultural competence in health care. *States of Health* 5(4):1–3, 1995.
3. Kohnert K., et al: Breadth and depth of diversity in Minnesota: Challenges to clinical competency. *American Journal of Speech-Pathology* 12:259–272, Aug. 2003.
4. The Center for Linguistic and Cultural Competence in Health Care: Glossary of terms. *Office of Minority Health Home Page*, U.S. Department of Health and Human Services, Mar. 4, 2003. www.omhrc.gov/cultural/glossary.htm (last accessed May 6, 2005).
5. Kagawa-Singer M., Kassim-Lakha S.: A strategy to reduce cross-cultural miscommunication and increase the likelihood of improving health outcomes. *Academic Medicine* 78(6):577–587, Jun. 2003.
6. Health Resources and Services Administration, U.S. Department of Health and Human Services: Bridging cultures and enhancing care: Approaches to cultural and linguistic competency in managed care. *Health Resources and Services Administration Home Page*, May 30, 2002. www.hrsa.gov/financeMC/bridging-cultures/ (last accessed May 10, 2005).
7. Smedley B.D., Stith A.Y., Nelson A.R. (eds.): *Unequal Treatment: Confronting Racial and Ethnic Disparities in Health Care.* Committee on Understanding and Eliminating Racial and Ethnic Disparities in Health Care. The National Academies Press. National Academy of Sciences, 2003.
8. Sedlis S.P., et al.: Racial differences in performance of invasive cardiac procedures in a department of veteran affairs medical center. *Journal of Clinical Epidemiology* 50(8):899–901, 1997.
9. Mitchell J.B., McCormack L.A.: Time trends in late stage diagnosis of cervical cancer: Differences by race/ethnicity and income. *Medical Care* 35(12):1220–1224, 1997.
10. Smith D.: *Health Care Divided; Race and Healing a Nation.* Ann Arbor, MI: University of Michigan Press, 1999.
11. Wintz S., Cooper E.P.: *Learning Module, Cultural and Spiritual Sensitivity: A Quick Guide to Cultures and Spiritual Traditions.* Association of Professional Chaplains, 2003.
12. Joint Commission Resources: *The Joint Commission Guide to Patient and Family Education.* Oakbrook Terrace, IL: Joint Commission Resources, 2003.
13. Joint Commission Resources: *Improving the Care Experience.* Oakbrook Terrace, IL: Joint Commission Resources, 2000.

14. Health Resources and Services Administration, U.S. Department of Health and Human Services: Cultural Competence Works: Using cultural competence to improve the quality of health care for diverse populations and add value to managed care arrangements, 2001. http://www.hrsa.gov/financeMC/ftp/cultural-competence.pdf#search='Cultural%20Competence%20Works' (last accessed May 10, 2005)

Three

The Role
of Community
in
Cultural Competence

As discussed in the previous chapter, organizational cultural competence requires a considerable understanding of the communities served and the ability to accurately plan for and implement services that respond to the cultural and linguistic characteristics of the organization's service area. In other words, there is more to cultural competence than simply striving for an acceptable level of patient satisfaction.

This chapter looks at the interrelationship of community and cultural competence. It explores the methods and benefits of involving individuals and institutions in health care programs and the importance of health promotion to the community. The pages ahead also describe the ways in which hiring and training can strengthen ties with the community, and outline the pivotal process of collecting data from the community to better respond to its health care needs.

Operating in an Environment of Community Inclusion

Health care organizations that are truly culturally competent are those that are seen as an extension of the communities they serve. Organizations that achieve this standing rely on the involvement of patients and community members in identifying community needs, assets, and barriers, and in creating appropriate program responses. In organizations that are truly culturally competent, patients and community members play an active role in needs assessment, program development, implementation, and evaluation.[1]

T ERMINOLOGY

Family/community inclusion is the participation of family members/entities or community-based networks in the development, implementation, and decision-making processes of health care delivery.[2]

I P
Through the process of inclusion, organizations are better able to examine the essential culturally based issues that affect service delivery and its outcome and, consequently, integrate more responsive approaches.

Distinguishing Family and Community Inclusion

Although family inclusion is more narrowly categorized as contributions made in or derived from specific health encounters, community inclusion refers to individual and institutional contributions across the service area. Inclusion assumes that through active and ongoing participation, individuals and networks can act as agents of change to facilitate improved social, behavioral, and health outcomes in individuals more effectively than a systems-based approach exclusively.[2]

Identifying the Characteristics of Community

In approaching community involvement in health care planning and delivery as an intervention, organizations are encouraged to isolate those characteristics of community that may have an impact on health outcomes. This involves considering questions such as the following:

- What are the characteristics of "community" that support or facilitate positive social and behavioral outcomes in health programs? Who are the appropriate representatives to involve? What level of involvement should be sought, at what points of the process, and over what period of time?
- Do specific attributes or mechanisms of community involvement have a measurable effect? What kinds of studies can be designed to measure the impact of community involvement on outcomes?
- What skills do health planners and providers need to successfully recruit community input and integrate that input into health planning and delivery?[2]

Desirable outcomes would include more routine involvement of community into program design and delivery, greater community acceptability, and participation in health programs.

Approaches to Involving Community in Health Care

Meeting the health care needs of a given community requires a collaborative process that is informed and influenced by that community's interests, expertise, and needs. When care and services are informed by the community's health care needs and are based in the community, then the community is invested in an organization and patients are

 I P
For some organizations, this relationship is forged through strategies that include inviting individuals from the community to serve as voting members of the organizations' governing boards.

more likely to use the services. This process of collaboration is also more likely to lead to more acceptable, responsive, efficient, and effective care.[3]

Organizations can gather community support,
input, and recommendations through the development
of community advisory boards, client panels, task
forces, or town meetings. They can sponsor locally
based community research (interviews, focus groups,
and so on), and integrate the results into their program
design.[3] Organizations can also integrate patients and
community members into their health care programming by drawing volunteers from the
target community to serve, for example, as peer advocates who help new clients negotiate the system.

I P
Organizations can build
relationships to improve
their quality of care by
seeking out various ways to
involve the community in
their health care system.

A health care organization in Newark, New Jersey, operates a Latino community health
center that addresses the needs of the city's growing Latino community. The center provides services to more than 5,000 patients annually and acts as a vehicle for conducting research to more effectively serve the Latino community.[4] Harborview Medical Center in
Seattle has established the Community House Calls/Caseworker Cultural Mediator
Program, where caseworker cultural mediators provide a wide range of services that include
interpretation, cultural mediation, case management, advocacy, follow up, coordination of
patient care, health education, home visits, and assistance in accessing English as a Second
Language and citizenship classes.[4]

Responding to Community Needs

Having a mechanism to assess community needs on an ongoing basis is as important as
it is in the initial stages of care, according to J. Carey Jackson, M.D., M.P.H., medical di-
rector of interpreter services at the Harborview Medical Center. For Harborview's
Community House Calls Program, feedback comes from a community advisory board.
"It is a way to form a dialogue between the community and the hospital," said Jackson.
"Our patients know right where to go to get a message to the hospital."[4]

Harborview launched the program in the early 1990s after realizing it was not serving
certain patients as well as it should. "We observed that when a patient had a bad experience, it reverberated through the community and people would stop showing up,"
explained Jackson. This program has enabled Harborview to raise the level of cultural
competency and customer service across the organization.

Building Committees of Diversity to Improve Cultural Competence

Organizations that form an advisory committee reflective of the community it serves are
establishing a vital management asset. As a direct link from the community to the organization, advisory committees can provide unique insight into the community and contribute practical advice in designing outreach activities and health promotion.

I P
Organizations should establish specific criteria for membership on such a committee, including special expertise or representation from particular groups. These members should be given a clear understanding of what their duties will encompass, the amount of time that will be required of them, and the particular expertise each person is being asked to contribute (such as marketing support, development of Spanish language materials, and engaging community contacts).[5]

Meetings of the committee should be scheduled at times and locations convenient for the members. Meeting agendas and reading materials should be distributed well in advance of each meeting to ensure maximum use of time and encourage attendance. Written progress reports can help keep the committee informed about its progress. It is also important to provide the advisory committee with information on the ways in which its input will be used, and to elicit the help of the committee in evaluating its impact on an organization's programming goals.

Advisory committees that reflect and include members of an organization's service area can play a crucial role in helping that organization go beyond slogans in its efforts to promote the value of diversity. The committees can act as the catalyst for developing concrete ways of exemplifying the benefits of diverse clientele, staff, board members, consultants, and volunteers.[5]

The contributions of an advisory committee might include ensuring that diverse people are depicted on agency brochures, that ethnic art is displayed in the facility's lobby, that certain cultural and religious holidays are acknowledged, or that efforts to recruit and retain diverse staff are continually being improved. It is important to be aware that for some people certain religious holidays, or holy days, require participation in rituals or worship, prohibit travel, or impact dietary or medication use.

Although research varies and further studies are needed, some studies have concluded that community inclusion as an intervention can do the following:

- Increase screening rates
- Assist medical providers in overcoming challenges in caring for elder patients
- Positively influence the participation of individuals in training programs
- Assure the cultural acceptability of research tools leading to higher response rates
- Increase access to information about the community[2]

Advisory committees can provide real-life contributions to an organization's promotion, execution, and evaluation of cultural competence.

Enhancing Health Promotion in the Community

Culturally competent health promotion (CCHP) incorporates culturally sensitive concepts and practices into health promotion activities.

ERMINOLOGY
Health promotion is the process by which individuals, communities, and populations are given the tools necessary to improve health outcomes.[6]

Health promotion through community relations and outreach includes community-based services, programs, and promotion such as health fairs, case management, public relations, and advocacy campaigns targeted at meeting the health and psychosocial needs of local community populations. Health promotion also involves partnerships with community-based resources and leaders as well as in-organization training and education for staff and clinicians on community needs and values.

The aim of CCHP is improving health outcomes by communicating healthy behaviors, encouraging early detection and treatment of disease, and educating the public on the care of chronic disease. Health promotion programs and activities are often most effective, however, when they appeal to the interests of the targeted communities. This can include such simple acts as ensuring that posters in an organization's waiting room include images of individuals of different ages and ethnicities.

Unique Examples of Culturally Competent Health Promotion

CCHP might also take the form of a community lunch or dinner, where community members are asked about their experiences and perceptions of health care. Through one organization, a group of women meets regularly at a Kansas City hotel conference center for lunch. They come for the food, the socializing, and the educational program.[6]

The Ladies' Lunch is part of the homeless outreach program offered by Swope Parkway Health Centers in Kansas City, Missouri. The program started as an HIV/AIDS education effort targeted to prostitutes and now includes other health issues, as well as AIDS, as the meeting focus. "The attendees set their own agenda," said E. Frank Ellis, chairman of Swope Parkway, which operates seven health centers in Kansas and Missouri. "They talk about what they want to talk about. It was our way of providing culturally specific information to this target base." The program has brought more members of this community into the HIV clinic and into the primary care clinic.

IP
Through culturally competent health promotion, organizations are able to improve health outcomes in the health care setting and in the community they serve.

> *T* I P
> Health care organizations can partner with faith-based or religious organizations to provide health promotion activities and essential information on possible cultural and religious needs that may arise.

Determining the Effect of Health Promotion Strategies

Questions that organizations should continue to consider when assessing the effectiveness of such promotional programs include the following:

- What is the impact of CCHP programs versus standard health promotion programs?
- Is the effect isolated to the receipt of the intervention itself or is it the cultural competence aspects of the intervention that make the difference?
- Do outcomes significantly improve when the intervention is highly tailored to subgroups and subcultures as opposed to generalized CCHP programs?[6]

> *T* I P
> Assessing the effectiveness of CCHP allows organizations to increase, improve, or modify their outreach efforts.

Expanding your Affiliations to Extend Cultural Competence

By combining forces with other local agencies, social service organizations, and even education and advocacy organizations, health care organizations can do more than increase CCHP, they can extend their culturally competent services.

These affiliations can begin as informational meetings between members of an organization's staff and representatives of these groups, or they might be as formal as co-sponsoring conferences and events. Such collaboration allows an organization to build meaningful relationships with the communities it serves, providing it with more insights about culturally influenced health behaviors and how best to meet the needs of these constituencies.

By expanding its affiliations, organizations can do the following:

- Develop relationships with other health organizations that have made efforts to develop culturally competent care
- Increase the visibility of their organization by co-sponsoring events in their community. Sign on with charity walks for breast cancer research or the American Heart Association. Contact the local medical school and find out if students have organized mobile clinics that the organization can contribute to with volunteers or supplies.
- Network and develop relationships with other organizations to create community-based task forces that reach specific populations in nonclinical settings (such as churches, barbershops, hair salons).

- Develop community-specific health information materials using focus groups, community meetings, and other means to collect neighborhood experiences, needs, and recommendations.[7]
- Create a shared vision of health care excellence with the community that draws on community experience to educate and guide practitioners and organizations in their understanding of the populations they are striving to serve. Talk to other nonprofit organizations in the area or poll clients about how their organization might better serve them.[7]

When the Family Health Care Center (FHC) in Fargo, North Dakota, began to serve a large new and diverse refugee community, FHC was a catalyst in the development of a medical interpretation training and provision program. The interpretation program is now operated independently, with many agencies and organizations using its services. Developing such a service in an area whose population previously consisted of a large Scandinavian American population and smaller Native American and Spanish-speaking migrant farm-worker populations has allowed local agencies to build an infrastructure that can adapt to and serve the many new refugees resettling in the area.[1]

I P
Community members may be hired as office staff, community health workers, outreach workers, and all levels of nursing staff.

Sidebar 3-1. Managing the Size and Diversity of Community Partnerships on page 74 focuses on how properly managed community health partnerships can achieve similarly successful outcomes.

Improving Competence by Employing Community Members

In addition to having community members serve on boards of directors, community advisory boards, and committees, many organizations make efforts to hire individuals from the community or from similar cultural, economic, and linguistic backgrounds as community members when looking to fill staff positions.[1]

Many organizations provide residency and training opportunities for minority providers. In any of the previously listed capacities, community members may provide direct services or act as cultural facilitators and interpreters between staff and clients. They can also serve as resources for training other staff.[1]

I P
Employing bilingual/bicultural people from the local community in project positions can make clients more comfortable. The ability to interact with another member of his or her own community can help a client feel more at ease in a health care setting.

Sidebar 3-1.
Managing the Size and Diversity of Community Partnerships

Community health partnerships need to attract a wide range of members to be seen as relevant and credible in their local communities. Partnerships that are successful in this are more likely, first of all, to build a broad membership base representing all sectors of the community. This includes the health sector (hospitals, insurers, health systems, and individual medical providers), social services sector (government and not-for-profit agencies focused on aging, mental health, housing, and welfare), the business community (local corporations and small businesses), local and state government leaders (mayors, city council and board of supervisors members, state representatives, cultural and religious centers), and community members.

Second, successful partnerships actively encourage diversity through grassroots involvement of consumers and target populations. For example, one rural partnership actively encouraged its clients to attend community forums to share their concerns. As a result, it learned that the community wanted help with the purchase of expensive medications for people with chronic illnesses. The partnership developed a medical assistance program to get medication into the hands of people who needed it. It also asked each client attending a health clinic to complete a satisfaction survey soliciting feedback and ideas for addressing community health problems. The governing council now uses this information when it makes policy decisions.

Third, the most effective partnerships intentionally seek political support for their causes by building relationships with local and state representatives. One rural partnership networked with its county board of supervisors and state agencies to draw attention to rural health issues and to the partnership's innovative programs and progress in serving the uninsured. As a result, the partnership has received grants of local and state funds for its programs.

Finally, successful partnerships use a wide range of methods and strategies to involve members in planning partnership priorities and activities and to sustain this involvement over time. For example, a rural partnership developed two separate councils to ensure the ongoing involvement of agencies and the broader community: An interagency council, which serves the target population, meets regularly to discuss partnership progress and encourage cross-sector collaboration. A community health council, designed to reach out to grassroots leaders and concerned community members, holds quarterly open forums to discuss the community's health concerns and needs.

Source: Greising Cynthia Hedges: Public-Private Partnerships to Improve Health Care: Summary of the Evaluation of the National Community Care Network Demonstration. *Health Research and Educational Trust Program (HRET) Home Page*. www.hret.org/hret/programs/commhlth.html (last accessed May 11, 2005). Used with permission.

$\mathcal{T}$ERMINOLOGY

Community health workers (CHWs) are typically members of a particular community tasked with improving the health of that community in cooperation with the health care system or public health agencies.[8]

Benefiting from Community Health Workers

Incorporating community members into the health care delivery system as community health workers can be a particularly effective way of bridging the gap between the service delivery system.

Community Health Workers as Change Agents

Working as agents of change, CHWs can provide a variety of services, including the following:

- Outreach to underserved and hard-to-reach populations
- Health promotion/disease prevention educational instruction
- Patient tracking
- Needs assessment and the provision of follow-up services
- Patient advocacy and assistance
- Limited health care services[8]

> ## $\mathcal{T}$IP
> Community health workers can serve as intermediaries, relaying the community's concerns to the program and, in turn, educating the community on health concerns and behaviors.

Although many of these services can be delivered through a direct systems-based approach, CHWs are often trained to provide these same services by integrating a more culturally and linguistically sensitive approach.

Facilitating Understanding Through Community Health Workers

In addition to being part of the existing community and social network, CHWs ideally possess certain skills and capacities that are essential to gaining the trust and acceptance of individuals. These can include cultural communication and mediation skills, an understanding of the community's health belief systems and knowledge of a community's strengths and capacities, and the ability to use effective approaches for reaching targeted individuals. Through an integrated approach, CHWs can facilitate a better understanding of the changes that are sought without threatening the interests or cultural values of the community.

While influencing health-related behavioral change and outcomes in targeted communities, CHWs can also assist systems and service providers by assessing the community's

I P
Distinguishing and understanding
alternative models and practices can be
useful in uncovering potential barriers to
service delivery while providing the
opportunity to integrate specific
components into conventional practice.[8]

cultural pulse. They can solicit information on community barriers, patterns of social interaction and decision making, past efforts aimed at changing health behaviors, and associated successes and failures. This information will enable providers and institutions to adopt methods that more effectively respond to the targeted community.

Integrating Special Practices that Respond to Community Needs

In many ethnic communities, health status, the causes of disease, and health care treatment may be defined or explained through traditional or folk methods or practices. For some, illness could be caused by injuries, environmental factors, interpersonal conflicts, witchcraft, sorcery, or spirits.[8] To people in some cultures, a particular illness might be seen as the result of violating cultural, religious, spiritual, or traditional norms. Responding to this cultural view often involves adjustments in conventional medicine and respectful consideration of traditional practices and remedies.

In cases that involve traditional beliefs, organizations can call on traditional healers to serve as consultants. In some cultures, the use of traditional practices/healers may be the first and only approach to dealing with health-related concerns. Other individuals may be more open to an integration of both traditional and conventional approaches. Organizations that employ board-certified, professional chaplains are able to focus directly on the significance and incorporation of cultural, spiritual, and religious practices into the plan of care.

Although more studies are needed on the subject, studies suggest the following:

- Traditional healers are consulted for common medical conditions
- Using alternative methods in conjunction with conventional methods can be an effective approach
- Patients are reluctant to inform physicians and other members of their community about the use of traditional practices/healers for fear of judgment and stigmatization[8]

I P
Organizations should actively involve professional health care pastoral care providers who are clinically trained and nationally board certified, ethnic community representatives, or traditional healers in assessing and initiating any programming that involves alternative medicines or therapies. Care providers must also be sensitive to concerns about testing the "efficacy" of alternate treatments or healers.

Using Data to Design Culturally Competent Care

An important aspect of involving community in the health care process involves data collection and measurement. To achieve successful provision of care, organizations must possess the capacity to identify the distinct communities they serve and, through research based on data, develop effective practices that respond to the unique barriers these communities face.

Chapter Five outlines the purposes and practices of collecting data as a performance measure in cultural competence programming, but in terms of gathering community information organizations can use intake databases to ensure that a client's cultural, linguistic, and personal background information is documented and considered in designing care. For example, the Multicultural Program of the Maricopa Integrated Health System uses a computerized intake program that captures language, ethnicity, and nationality data used for program management. Treatment plans, including discharge planning and follow up, include cultural needs and involve the patient and family.[1]

Several programs examine morbidity and mortality data available for the population or for similar populations and are also active in developing their own baseline data for the specific local populations they serve. They also compare that data with similar populations elsewhere.

I P
Through the effective use of data, organizations are able to both measure and design effective cultural competence programming.

Data Collection and the Care of the Community

With evidence from the last 20 years showing that racial, ethnic, and language-based disparities remain present in health care,[9] measurement and outcomes have become increasingly important for demonstrating the value of health care. As stated in the IOM report "Unequal Treatment: Confronting Racial and Ethnic Disparities in Health Care":

The real challenge lies not in debating whether disparities exist, but in developing and implementing strategies to reduce and eliminate them. Confronting such "unequal treatment" will require a broad and sustained commitment from those who provide care, as well as those who receive it.[9]

If data on race, ethnicity, primary language, and information regarding values and beliefs are available, disparities in health care can be addressed through a quality of care framework.[10] Sidebar 3-2. Why Collect Racial and Ethnic Health Care Data? on page 78 expands on the reasons for such data collection.

I P
Clearly, data collection and analysis can play a pivotal role in improving the quality of care provided to vulnerable populations.

Sidebar 3-2.
Why Collect Racial and Ethnic Health Care Data?

- Evaluate and monitor effectiveness of programs
- Understand etiologic process and identify differences in performance within a plan
- Design targeted quality improvement activities
- Develop cost-effective improvement efforts
- Identify the need for and deploy resources for the provision of culturally and linguistically appropriate services
- Monitor trends over time at local, state, and national levels
- Help all parties understand the scope of the problem of health disparities affecting their clients and stimulate action
- Empower consumers to make informed decisions about health plan choice
- Ensure civil rights

Source: Health Resources and Services Administration, U.S. Department of Health and Human Services: Bridging cultures and enhancing care: Approaches to cultural and linguistic competency in managed care. *Health Resources and Services Administration Home Page*, May 30, 2002. www.hrsa.gov/financeMC/bridging-cultures/ (last accessed May 10, 2005).

Most hospitals (82%) currently collect data on their patients' race and ethnicity, and 67% collect information on patients' primary language.[10] However, the data are not always collected in a systematic or standard manner and are often not shared, even within different departments in the same hospital.

Gaining Tools and Resources on Data Collection

With the recent announcement by the Department of Health and Human Services that the federal government will implement a national electronic medical record system in 10 years, and with 22 states mandating the collection of race and ethnicity data, the need for standardization has become increasingly urgent, according to the Health Research and Educational Trust (HRET). With the support of the Commonwealth Fund, HRET has developed a new Web-based toolkit for hospitals and other

I P
Organizations that collect accurate data can use the information obtained to ensure they have sufficient language assistance services, develop appropriate patient education materials, and track quality indicators and health outcomes for specific groups to inform improvements in quality of care.[10]

health care providers to collect race, ethnicity, and primary language information (the toolkit can be accessed by going to www.hretdisparities.org).

The aim of the toolkit is to help hospitals collect accurate information from patients to meet regulatory and local community demands. Hospitals can use the data to monitor health care delivery and quality of care by linking to clinical measures and targeting appropriate interventions to specific groups. Sidebar 3-3. Collecting Detailed Data on Race and Ethnicity on page 80 expands on the HRET's data collection design.

Before asking patients to provide information about their racial and ethnic background, the HRET toolkit recommends providing patients with a rationale for why this information is being sought. Research conducted with patients at Northwestern University showed that they were most comfortable providing this information when told that it was being used for "monitoring quality of care for everyone."[10]

According to the HRET toolkit, it is also important to point out to patients that "the only people who see this information are registration staff, administrators for the hospital, and the people involved in quality improvement and oversight, and the confidentiality of what you say is protected by law."[10]

The toolkit provides both the OMB and CDC Race and Ethnicity Code Sets and points out that under the CDC Code Sets guidelines, health care providers have permission to ask completely open-ended questions, allowing patients to "use their own words," and then aggregate this more detailed information into broader categories for analytical purposes. This process enables a hospital to collect more granular information, which may be more useful in planning for interpreter services, developing patient education materials, and understanding patient dietary needs. Table 3.1: "Staff Training Question and Answer Response Matrix Presentation" on pages 81 and 82 illustrates this question and answer model.

Putting Data into Practice

Eliminating racial and ethnic disparities in health care is a central issue in overall efforts to improve and sustain quality of care. Information on racial and ethnic characteristics of the U.S. population is needed to target quality improvement efforts, identify the nature and extent of disparities, and monitor progress. Measurement, reporting, and benchmarking are critical to improving care. In addition, legal statutes and laws require reporting data by race and ethnicity to monitor discriminatory practices.

By investing in effective and ongoing staff training, health care organizations are better positioned to collect data accurately and consistently, and providers are better equipped to put new approaches based on data results into action.

 I P
Hospitals and other health care organizations need to be responsive to the communities they serve and a first step toward accomplishing this goal is understanding who the community is and working collaboratively to address problems and concerns.

Sidebar 3-3.
Collecting Detailed Data on Race and Ethnicity

The recently released report by the National Research Council of the National Academies, "Eliminating Health Disparities: Measurement and Data Needs," recommends that hospitals and health insurers collect standardized data on race and ethnicity using the Office of Management and Budget (OMB) standards as a base minimum. However, experts recognize that greater detail or granularity beyond the OMB categories may be more useful for hospitals and health care organizations. Therefore, it is recommended to capture more detailed data on race and ethnicity, which can be aggregated to the broader OMB categories for reporting purposes.

HRET recommends collecting race and ethnicity information directly from patients. This information should be collected only once and periodically validated. Repeated collection should be avoided to reduce the burden both for patients and for staff responsible for collecting the information. After this information is collected, it should be stored in an electronic format when possible.

Two primary components of race and ethnicity data collection should be considered standard practice: (1) data should be collected directly from the patient or from a designated representative, and (2) a reason should be provided for why this information is being collected.

HRET recommends using an open-ended format for collecting race and ethnicity information from patients so patients can use their own words and define up to four racial/ethnic categories. This method has been successfully implemented at Northwestern Memorial Hospital in Chicago. It takes, on average, just 38 seconds to complete data collection using this format. However, we recognize that not all hospitals may be able to implement a system for data collection using an open-ended format. Therefore, we provide information for using the broader OMB categories as well as the more detailed Centers for Disease Control (CDC) Race and Ethnicity Code Sets.

Source: Health Research and Educational Trust (HRET): A toolkit for collecting race, ethnicity, and primary language information from patients. *Health Research and Educational Trust (HRET) Home Page.* www.hretdisparities.org/hretdisparities/index.jsp (last accessed May 11, 2005). Used with permission.

As the next chapter discusses in detail, staff training in cultural and linguistic competence is a crucial component in positioning health care organizations to respond to the needs of the communities they serve, and to work to reduce health disparities.

Table 3.1
Staff Training Question and Answer Response Matrix Presentation

Patient Response Matrix—Routine			
Patient Response	Suggested Response	Hints	Code
"I'm American."	"Would you like to use an additional term, or would you like me to put American?"		American or others if specified
"Can't you tell by looking at me?"	"Well, usually, I can. But sometimes I'm wrong, so we think it is better to let people tell us."		
If using open-ended option: "I don't know. What are the responses?"	"You can say White, Black or African-American, Latino or Hispanic, Asian, American Indian or Alaskan Native, Pacific Islander or Native Hawaiian, some other race, or any combination of these. You can also use more specific terms like Irish, Jamaican, Mexican."		
"I was born in Nigeria, but I've really lived here all my life. What should I say?"	"That is really up to you. You can use any term you like. It is fine to say that you are Nigerian."	It's best not to ask for this information again.	
Patients Returning			
A patient returning for care with the Refusal code.	DO NOT ASK AGAIN.		
A patient returning for care with the "UN" or "Unable to provide information" code.	Proceed to ask for the information per routine.		
Tougher Questions—continued			
"I'm human."	"Is that your way of saying that you don't want to answer the question? If so, I can say that you didn't want to answer."	DON'T SAY "I'll just code as a refusal."	Refusal

(continued)

Table 3.1—continued

Tougher Questions—continued			
Patient Response	Suggested Response	Hints	Code
"It's none of your business."	"I'll put down that you didn't want to answer, which is fine."	DON'T SAY "I'll just code as a refusal."	Refusal
"Why do you care? We're all human beings."	"Well, lots of studies from around the country have shown that a patient's race and ethnicity can affect how they get treated. We want to make sure that doesn't happen here, so we use this information to check and make sure that everyone gets the best care possible. If we find a problem, we fix it."	If patient still refuses, DON'T SAY "I'll just code as a refusal."	Refusal
"Are you saying that this has happened at _____?"	"No. As best we know, everyone gets the same excellent care here. But, we want to make sure that this never happens in the future."		
"Who looks at this?"	"The only people who see this information are registration staff, administrators for the hospital and the people involved in quality improvement and oversight."		
"Are you trying to find out if I'm a U.S. citizen?"	"No. Definitely not! Also, you should know that the confidentiality of what you say is protected by law."		

What if the patient presents a race/ethnicity that's not on the table?

- Code as "Other."
- Staff should flag this (e.g. record this information); if this happens frequently, it may indicate a new category that needs to be added to the coding scheme.

**Provide contact information of "point person"
for any questions or concerns that may come up.**

Source: Health Research and Educational Trust (HRET): A toolkit for collecting race, ethnicity, and primary language information from patients. *Health Research and Educational Trust (HRET) Home Page.* www.hretdisparities.org/hretdisparities/index.jsp (last accessed May 11, 2005). Used with permission.

References

1. Health Resources and Services Administration, U.S. Department of Health and Human Services: Cultural Competence Works: Using cultural competence to improve the quality of health care for diverse populations and add value to managed care arrangements, 2001. http://www.hrsa.gov/ financeMC/ftp/cultural-competence.pdf#search='Cultural%20Competence%20Works' (last accessed May 10, 2005)

2. Resources for Cross Cultural Health Care, the U.S. Department of Health and Human Services Office of Minority Health, and the Agency for Healthcare Research and Quality: Developing a research agenda for cultural competence in health care: Family/Community inclusion in health care delivery, *Diversity RX Home Page*, Nov. 13, 2001. www.diversityrx.org/HTML/RCPROJ_F.htm (last accessed May 12, 2005).

3. National Public Health and Hospital Institute: *Serving Diverse Communities in Hospital and Health Systems*. U.S. Department of Health and Human Services. Nov. 2003.

4. Rollins G.: Customer service: Creating community connections to exceed expectations. *The Safety Net* pp. 17–18, Fall 2003.

5. National CASA Association: Cultural competence in your program. *CASANet Resources Home Page*. www.casanet.org/program-management/diversity/cultural-competence.htm (last accessed May 11, 2005).

6. Resources for Cross Cultural Health Care, the U.S. Department of Health and Human Services Office of Minority Health, and the Agency for Healthcare Research and Quality: Developing a research agenda for cultural competence in health care: Culturally competent health promotion. *DiversityRX Home Page*, Nov. 13, 2001. www.diversityrx.org/HTML/RCPROJ_C.htm (last accessed May 9, 2005).

7. Second national conference on quality health care for culturally diverse populations: Strategy and action for communities, providers, and a changing health system, Oct. 11–14, 2000, *DiversityRX Home Page*. diversityrx.org/CCCONF/00/00_proc_03.htm#A (last accessed May 10, 2005).

8. Resources for Cross Cultural Health Care, the U.S. Department of Health and Human Services Office of Minority Health, and the Agency for Healthcare Research and Quality: Developing a research agenda for cultural competence in health care: Community health workers. *DiversityRX Home Page*, Nov. 13, 2001. www.diversityrx.org/HTML/RCPROJ_D.htm (last accessed May 11, 2005).

9. Smedley B.D., Stith A.Y., Nelson A.R. (eds.): *Unequal Treatment: Confronting Racial and Ethnic Disparities in Health Care*. Committee on Understanding and Eliminating Racial and Ethnic Disparities in Health Care. The National Academies Press. National Academy of Sciences, 2003.

10. Health Research and Educational Trust (HRET): A toolkit for collecting race, ethnicity, and primary language information from patients. *Health Research and Educational Trust (HRET) Home Page*. www.hretdisparities.org/hretdisparities/index.jsp (last accessed May 11, 2005).

Four

Developing and
Training Staff
to be
Culturally Competent

An American Indian patient lies in the intensive care unit (ICU), feeling cut off from all he understands about healing. According to his culture, a sick person's room must be purified by burning a bundle of sage leaves, "smudging" the space as well as the patient and all who enter the room by outlining them with a wand of fragrant smoke before any healing can happen. A small bag, brought by the medicine man of his tribe, needs to stay with him at all times and he wants his family there. The sterility, isolation, and machinery of the modern ICU are the alien apparatus of a culture that can only take away his spirit, not give it back. He refuses treatment.[1]

In confronting health care disparities and addressing the increasing racial and ethnic diversity of the U.S. population, the development and implementation of cultural competence training programs for health care providers has emerged as a key intervention strategy. Cross-cultural education programs, another term for this type of training, are viewed as a means to enhance health professionals' awareness of how cultural and social factors influence health care. Effective training programs promote and provide methods to obtain, negotiate, and clinically manage this information.

This chapter reveals great progress and serious challenges in the areas of cultural competence and medical interpretation training. The chapter reviews the variety of training approaches and programming, outlines the settings and services, examines training curricula and methods of measurement, considers the contribution of health care leaders to effective training, and assesses the need to standardize training methodologies.

Determining the Boundaries of Cultural Competence Training

In the past, the diversity training of most health care organizations consisted of an organizational audit and education about equal employment opportunity and affirmative action regulations. Cross-cultural training can now be divided into three conceptual approaches focusing on attitudes (cultural sensitivity/awareness approach), knowledge (multicultural/categorical approach), and skills (cross approach). These approaches have been taught using a variety of interactive and experiential methodologies.[3]

$\mathcal{T}$ERMINOLOGY

Cross-cultural or cultural competence training is a vast array of educational activities aimed at enhancing the capacity of the service delivery system to meet the needs of different racial and ethnic populations.[2]

Cultural competence training can include educational activities aimed at increasing sensitivity and awareness, the provision of multicultural health and demographic information on service area populations, skills building in bicultural and bilingual interviewing and patient assessment, enhancing the use of race or ethnic-specific epidemiological data in diagnosis and treatment, and increasing cultural knowledge and understanding.

$\mathcal{T}$ I P
The knowledge gained through training allows providers and institutions to develop new and better approaches to communication, patient care, and services planning pertaining to culture and language.[2]

Considering Standards in Training

One study linking sociocultural factors and the clinical encounter included expert suggestions that training—which may include education in cultural competence for senior management, health care providers, and staff—should focus on knowledge, skills, and self-awareness of their own beliefs and values. It should also equip providers to deliver quality care to all patients. The study stressed, however, that systems must be in place to facilitate this goal. Curricula should be standardized and evidence based, with appropriate monitoring to ensure completion (such as taking courses as part of being in a provider network, as a way of distinguishing health plans, or as part of licensure). Curricula, furthermore, must be devoid of stereotypes in their descriptions of ethnic group characteristics.[4]

Research has demonstrated that training can be effective in improving provider knowledge of cultural and behavioral aspects of health care and building effective communication strategies. Despite progress in the field, however, some believe the most significant challenges to realizing the potential of cross-cultural education strategies include the need to define educational core competencies, reach consensus on approaches and methodologies, determine methods of integration into the medical and nursing curriculum, and develop and implement appropriate evaluation strategies.[3]

$\mathcal{T}$ I P
Training should also incorporate socioeconomic factors, communication skills, and mechanisms for addressing racism and bias.

These steps would address what is considered to be an imbalance in cultural education. In academic settings, cultural competence training can range from semester-long courses to discrete components that are part of a broader course outline. Outside academic settings, continuing education courses, and courses designed for organizations and staff can range from a few hours to a few days.[3] The model curriculum used by professional, board-certified chaplains includes not only teaching through orientation and classes, but is enhanced by ongoing unit or department-based in-services for clinical and medical staff to provide continuity with updated information, resources, and support. This is especially effective in organizations where it is difficult to have direct care providers, such as nurses, be away from their units for lengthy or multiple training sessions.

The Advantages of Teaching Universal Skills

Each trainer develops his or her own content and teaching approach, and both content and approach vary widely. For example, a common method of teaching cultural competence is to provide a general overview of the role of culture in health service delivery, and then to spend time focusing on the health beliefs and behaviors of specific ethnic groups.

Although this has the effect of increasing general knowledge about an ethnic population, it can too easily lead to a form of stereotyping if improperly conducted or understood.

*T*I P
Teaching a more universal skills approach to cultural competence allows practitioners to use general questioning and medical history–taking techniques on any individual from any ethnic background, which is considered to be a more useful approach for health facilities that see a diverse clientele.[5] This skill could be combined with intensive education about specific ethnic groups.

Successful Approaches to Cultural Competence Training

Although these challenges continue to be considered in the field, many organizations approach training in cultural competence and medical interpretation with the same seriousness as training in other essential clinical skills. They have worked to establish hiring and training practices on a more professional level by doing the following:

- Developing specific hiring qualifications and mandated training requirements for all staff in language, medical interpretation, and cultural competence as their positions necessitate
- Producing a comprehensive and replicable training curriculum and qualifying factors
- Allocating the budget, resources, and time for staff training, including training for new staff, annual updates and review, as well as testing and job application criteria[6]

Organizations can provide internal training programs or rely on outside sources to facilitate training programs that are also open to other agencies and organizations. The Community Health Education Center (CHEC) of the Massachusetts Department of Public Health in Boston provides ongoing training and professional development opportunities to outreach educators through a Comprehensive Outreach Education Certificate Program. This program's training sessions include leadership development, assessment techniques, cultural competence, public health, outreach methods, cross-cultural communication, and design of educational materials. The CHEC's model, which will soon be replicated statewide, mixes localized knowledge into its core coursework.[6]

With limited resources as a barrier to maintaining cultural competence training, organizations can seek out the resources of area colleges and universities. Erlanger Health System in Chattanooga, Tennessee, surveyed its employees to determine what tools and training were needed for them to better communicate with a growing number of Spanish-speaking patients. The feedback led to a cost-effective partnership with nearby Chattanooga State Technical College. In exchange for a minimum number of participants, Chattanooga State developed a medically oriented Spanish course in collaboration with a Latino physician, who also serves as instructor. In addition to the basics of Spanish, the course addresses cultural considerations and population-specific medical concerns. Three higher-level classes have been developed since 2003 to make room for a steady flow of interested participants.[7]

 I P
Educational programs should constantly look for strategies to help them understand the needs of and ensure quality service to new cultural groups or emerging populations. The most culturally appropriate programs tend to be community-specific rather than ethnic group general.[6]

Conferences and workshops on cultural competence topics are another way that skills, resources, and training are conveyed. They include meetings designed for specific clinical settings (such as immunization programs or managed care organizations), specific ethnic group health characteristics and issues, and health status/condition-specific topics (such as ethno-geriatric medicine, maternal and child health, or HIV).[5]

Training models that stress the importance of learning about individuals and communities can guide staff in appropriate ways to approach cultural and linguistic differences in multiple communities. These learning-based models of cultural competence can be enhanced to include community- and culture-specific models. They may also be adapted to new populations. This is particularly important because many organizations serve multiple cultural or language groups.[6]

Again, not only must these approaches take into account that what is appropriate for a Hispanic population of New York City may not be for a Hispanic population in Dallas, but also that the needs, beliefs, and behaviors within a particular group may vary as well.

Examining the Curricula of Cross-Cultural Training

Most experts agree it is imperative that providers, clinicians, and health care staff understand and embrace the importance of building personal and organizational cultural and linguistic competency. One research paper that did evaluate the effectiveness of a particular training program found it to be of significant benefit to participants.

This training, conducted in Florida in June 2001 and entitled "An Overview and Evaluation of Cultural Competence Training for Public Health Professionals,"[8] also detailed the program's curricula, format, and measurement methods. The training program was a joint effort between the Florida Department of Health and the Institute of Public Health at Florida A&M University. The goal of this training was to increase the participants' knowledge of cultural competence and its relevance in improving the health status of the citizens of Florida.

The project was conducted in three phases. The first phase involved developing a training curriculum and materials. The curriculum focused on two primary areas: culture and its relationship to health, and the Conceptual Framework for the Provision of Culturally Competent Services in Public Health Settings. The second phase implemented the trainings. The third phase evaluated the training project on two levels: process and impact. Six trainings were conducted throughout the state. Each session lasted one full day.

Participants in the training included professionals from county health departments and minority community-based organizations that receive funding from the Florida Department of Health. Several different measures indicated that the training was a success and that participants gained valuable information about culture and cultural competence. An adapted version of this study is reprinted in Appendix A: An Overview and Evaluation of Cultural Competence Training for Public Health Professionals.

The authors of this training study noted that, individually, its results should be viewed with some skepticism because of the lack of a comparison group. However, when reviewing the results collectively, the training was deemed to be overwhelmingly successful.

Additional Recommendations

Based on the results of the evaluation of this project, the authors recommend expanding trainings based on the observation that participants seemed to have acquired a strong understanding of culture, but not enough cultural competence.[8]

Based on the analysis of the "Contract with Myself," the key points that participants indicated that they learned most were about culture. According to the authors, these results indicate that participants were so struck by the definition of race and ethnicity that they never moved to the next level of understanding cultural competence. A second full day of training, they contend, would allow for further exploration of and skill development in cultural competence. In addition, the authors suggest that increasing training frequency would allow for broader participation and greater dissemination of knowledge.

The authors' second recommendation is to make training such as this mandatory or readily available for all public health professionals.

Gaining the Support of Leadership in Cultural Competence Training

Persuading staff and organizations to undertake cultural competence training is not always an easy task. Health professionals often do not like to sit for long cultural competence training sessions unless they are required by credentialing bodies or by the organizations for which they work. When staff members do participate, they can be frustrated attempting to practice new skills in what may still be a culturally incompetent organization.

Some organizations resist taking time for organizationwide training. The reasons for their reluctance can range from cost and disruption to the discomfort of facing certain realities about their institution that training might not completely address.[5]

Buy-in from the CEO and board of directors of an organization can be a significant factor in whether employees embrace cultural competence training. One organization's board of directors adopted a three-year diversity plan in which a portion of executive management compensation is based on achieving cultural competence objectives. Some argue that leadership support of cultural competence should go beyond broad objectives to include participation. Senior executives at one health care agency attend leadership symposia that focus on diversity.[7]

Questioning the Trends in Cultural Competence Training

As public health agencies continue to address racial and ethnic health disparities, the need for cultural competence is becoming more clear. Many organizations have begun to move forward with training initiatives on the belief that the provision of cultural competence training can result in staff beginning to learn the concepts of cultural competence that will enable them to develop and apply appropriate knowledge and skills. As in the case of medical interpretation training for staff, questions remain about whether and which curricula models should be standardized throughout the field.

Many recommendations to health care organizations seeking to establish or improve cultural competence training focus on the need to examine the process as a whole. Some recommendations include the following:

- Support consensus development and adoption of cultural competence definitions and corresponding competencies for health professionals, including curriculum elements. Promote to providers, provider organizations, health profession associations, health profession educators, and cultural competence trainers.
- Assist with developing and implementing cultural competence course modules or courses into the health profession curricula. Promote to health profession educators, administrators, and state agencies overseeing health profession education and certification.
- Support placement of health profession students and prospective students in internships at health facilities expert in serving multicultural populations. Include a didactic cross-cultural health education component.
- Consider certifying cultural competence trainers from within all professional health care disciplines.
- Support synthesis of critical elements and techniques of cultural competence training programs.

- Disseminate information about model training programs.
- Support cultural competence training and developing cultural profiles and resources materials for health professionals, especially on topics related to the needs of recent newcomer groups.
- Promote health professional and provider organization interaction with local ethnic communities to learn more about community needs and health issues (such as ethnic community clinical advisory boards or ethnic/cross-cultural grand rounds).
- Support research and consensus development on whether widespread cultural competence assessment of health professionals is desirable and whether such testing, as a part of certification and accreditation, is feasible.[5]

 I P
It is essential that organizations use training materials and formats that are applicable to their unique needs. With board-certified chaplains on staff, the organization has educators familiar with the organization's mission, staff, patient population, and application issues readily available.

According to a report by the Office of Minority Health and the Agency for Healthcare Research and Quality,[2] the majority of the current literature encompasses descriptive studies of cultural competency training; its delivery approaches and techniques, arguments for using training as a means to eliminate disparities, and surveys of the prevalence of training in different educational settings. The content of training described in these studies varied widely and, the report notes, it is difficult to discern whether different approaches or content resulted in better post-training outcomes, or whether these variations have a subsequent impact on behavior.

Evaluating the Impact of Training on Participants

The Office of Minority Health and the Agency for Healthcare Research and Quality report also looked at studies that attempt to answer questions related to the impact of training on trainees and subsequent outcomes. In an effort to quantify the impact of training on trainees, these studies examined levels of cultural knowledge, attitudes, awareness, satisfaction, and communication skills.

According to the report, studies that empirically measured the impact of training found that self-assessments indicated significant increases in levels of cultural knowledge, attitudes, and awareness in both single and comparative groups. However, nonsubjective measures found that knowledge improved in some areas but not in others, and that there were modest improvements in some attitudes and few improvements in communication skills. Despite findings such as this, incorporating self-assessment issues into training is considered by many to be substantially more important than not addressing them at all.[2]

Studies that examined the impact of training on sensitivity generated inconclusive and often contradictory results. Several comparative studies attempted to determine the impact

I P

Organizations should be aware that additional research is needed to determine whether the standardization of cultural competence education is appropriate and effective and how established goals and objectives can be empirically measured to determine the best approaches for attaining identified outcomes.

and effectiveness of variations in training presentation and content. These studies reported different levels of effectiveness. However, others found no difference when measured empirically.

Assessing the Impact of Training on Care

The Office of Minority Health and the Agency for Healthcare Research and Quality found very few studies that examined the impact of training on patient behavior change or health outcomes and concluded that a need exists to define which are the most desirable outcomes from the patient-provider relationship, and which are the most reliable indicators of positive improvements that could result from training.[2]

Preparing Those Who Teach Cultural Competence

Those who lead cultural competency programs must have the benefit of continuing professional education and training in cultural competency. Greater emphasis is being placed on the role of faculty development in creating successful cultural competency education programs, which suggests that faculty must not only learn about the content for cultural competency curricula but they must also possess the skills to effectively facilitate candid discussions on sensitive topics such as racism and stereotypes.

One approach to prepare multidisciplinary groups of health professionals to teach cultural competence has been referred to as the training of trainers. The training of trainers approach relies on experiential and simulation techniques to influence attitudes and transfer knowledge and skills to participants.

I P

The scientific base supporting the use of cultural competency education and training assumes that positive impacts on trainees will result in behavioral changes that will facilitate the delivery of culturally competent care. It also assumes that these changes will eventually translate into improvements in health outcomes.[2] However, a clear need exists to examine and validate each of these assumptions as well as the types of education that have the most effective impact on outcomes in care.

Understanding the Training Methods for Medical Interpretation

Bilingual skills do not automatically make an individual an effective interpreter. Take the example of the provider who gives a non–English-speaking patient a prescription, explaining that it is for some suppositories. The interpreter is too embarrassed to admit that he does not know the equivalent word for "suppository" in the patient's language, so he uses the word for "pill" instead. The patient takes the medication orally and ends up in the emergency room.

In another case, a doctor asks his patient a question. The interpreter and the patient get into a long discussion, while the doctor sits and waits, completely left out. Finally the interpreter turns to the doctor and says, "She said no." When the doctor asks exactly what the patient said, the interpreter smiles and says, "Oh, it wasn't important. She just means no."[9]

 I P
Programs such as the training of trainers model are considered effective in faculty development because they emphasize program design and instructional facilitation techniques for teaching others.

Elements of Quality Interpretation

Quality interpretation includes sufficient proficiency in both languages, including mastery of the medical terminology in both languages. Trained interpreters have critically important memory skills, the ability to negotiate a three-way conversation, a self-awareness of one's own values and beliefs and how that impacts the process of interpretation, and basic knowledge of cultural attributes that can influence health.[10]

Because interpretation in the health care setting is a specialized skill and requires formalized training, uniform standards for both training and practice are prerequisites for high-quality translation. Yet, currently training programs have no minimum requirements, and many communities lack access to medically specific interpreter training programs. This lack of training can compromise the quality of the health care encounter.[10] It can also tarnish the reputation of qualified, properly trained interpreters when errors are made in translation.

The Various Structures of Medical Interpreter Training Programs

Medical interpreter training programs are being offered by hospitals, community-based organizations, language agencies, and a few institutions of higher education. However, these programs can vary widely in structure and quality because the field lacks consistent standards for training or certification. Training programs tend to fall into one of the following categories:

- Eight hours of instruction without testing
- A language proficiency test followed by less than one day of instruction
- Two days of instruction, occasionally accompanied by a practicum
- Forty hours or more of instruction with a practicum and a final exam (with or without a preceding language proficiency test)
- A combination of medical and court interpreter training
- One semester at the community college level with a practicum
- More than one semester at the college level
- Advanced degrees in interpreting.[10]

I P
Medical interpreting training programs should culminate in an oral test and a practicum where interpreters can actually practice what they have learned.

The National Council on Interpreting in Health Care (NCIHC) emphasizes the importance of establishing minimum criteria for a standardized medical interpreting training program. Training programs should consist of a minimum of 40 hours of instruction and include the following topic areas: medical terminology, interpreting skills, code of ethics or self-awareness of one's own values and beliefs, role-play, and cultural awareness.[11]

Testing a Model for Interpreter Training Curricula

Several challenges emerge when trying to develop standards and certification for interpreters. With the diversity in languages, creating proficiency tests for all languages is a daunting task, particularly for some of the less-familiar languages. Research is needed to determine what the average level of proficiency is for speakers of a certain language to evaluate how the use of common protocols and frameworks will affect them. Standards that are too rigid might reduce or eliminate the pool of qualified people available to serve as interpreters.[10]

Some organizations, such as the Massachusetts Medical Interpreters Association and the California Healthcare Interpreters Association (CHIA), have issued standards of practice for their states. See Figure 4-1. CHIA's *Standards of Practice* on page 97.

Ultimately, the goal of the *Standards of Practice* is to contribute to the acceptance of health care interpreting as a recognized profession, with the aim that this will lead to sustainable financing mechanisms and satisfactory reimbursement policies.[12]

The California Endowment has invested more than $15 million to ensure equal access for limited English proficiency (LEP) consumers. One of its various strategies focuses on improving the training and professionalization of medical interpreters. In addition to funding CHIA for the creation of the *Standards of Practice*, it has supported developing interpreter training curricula for community colleges and community-based organizations and a compendium of interpreter training programs in California, which includes an analysis of trends in the state.

 I P
At minimum, standards of certification for interpreters must also include an understanding of the medical environment, including how illness and injury impact patient/family beliefs, values, self-image, relationships, and the ability to communicate and receive information.[12]

Recognizing the Benefits of Medical Interpretation Training

Despite the slow progress in developing national standards and testing for medical interpretation, the field of training has advanced considerably.

Communicating Interpreter Roles and Expectations

For interpreters to function well in medical and social services environments, providers must understand the interpreter role and how to interact with

---

Figure 4-1.
CHIA's *Standards of Practice*

CHIA's *Standards of Practice* consists of three main sections that guide interpreters through the complex task of health care interpreting. The sections include the following:

Section 1: Ethical Principles—This section consists of six ethical principles that guide the actions of health care interpreters. Each principle has an underlying value description followed by a set of performance measures that demonstrate how the interpreter's action follows the principle.

Section 2: Protocols—This section describes procedures standardizing how interpreters work with patients and providers in the health care encounter before, during, and after their interaction or session.

Section 3: Complex Roles—This section describes four roles interpreters can play in the health care encounter and highlights strategies for setting appropriate boundaries.[12]

Source: California Healthcare Interpreters Association (CHIA): California Standards for Healthcare Interpreters: Ethical Principles, Protocols, and Guidance on Roles and Intervention. Los Angeles: 2002. Used with permission.

---

interpreters. Expectations about how information is communicated and, for example, whose responsibility it is to clarify complicated subjects or patient cultural concerns must be understood.[11] Clinical and administrative staff should be instructed or briefed on these issues in advance of the encounter.

At the University of Massachusetts Medical Center, defining interpreter roles and expectations is part of each new employee's orientation, and is included in orientation for medical students and residents. With funding from the United States Office of Health and Human Service (HHS) Office of Minority Health, Asian Health Services of Oakland developed and distributes a training packet for provider education on medical interpretation that incorporates lecture, role-play, supplementary readings, and a pre- and post-training test.[10] However, many settings introduce interpreters into the clinical or patient services environment without staff preparation. This can breed resentment and low utilization.

Including Functional Content in Medical Interpretation Training

The content of provider training for medical interpretation may include the following functional issues:

- Understanding provider responsibilities for communication
- Ethics
- Liability
- Triadic relationship
- Interpreter role and skills
- Negotiating basic cultural issues[13]

TIP
The development of uniform standards in medical interpretation training should lead to certification requirements that support the recognition of health care interpreting as a respected profession and an integral part of the health care team.[10]

Provider training should also include raising awareness about the impact of language barriers on patient care, and the factors involved in adequate communication, such as knowing when to call for an interpreter and not using family members.

As discussed in Chapter One, many organizations look to bilingual/bicultural members of the community to fill the important role of medical interpreter. Sidebar 4-1. Training Interpreters, Changing Lives on page 99 illustrates the benefits of reaching out to those who are already equipped with some important tools of the trade.

Chapter Five continues to consider the contribution of cultural competence to equal access and quality care. Its focus, however, is on assessing cultural competence's contribution to the bottom line. After all, although motivated by conviction and compassion, every health care organization faces the challenge of cost.

T I P
Organizations can incorporate the content of provider training for medical interpretation into its overall cultural competence training for professionals and staff, either in-house or in continuing education. Ideally, this content should be part of the health profession's education process.[12]

Sidebar 4.1
Training Interpreters, Changing Lives

The Medical Interpretation Training Program at Cambridge College in Cambridge, Massachusetts, grew out of a focus group about employment. Janis Peterson, who at the time worked for a community group, invited residents of one of the poorest neighborhoods in Cambridge to discuss their ideas about employment, job training, and education.

"We had a great number of people who spoke two, three, or even four languages. Many were health care professionals in their native countries, but here, they were working as house cleaners, cafeteria workers, and taxi drivers. Their language skills were being totally under-utilized," said Peterson, who is now coordinator of community collaborations at Cambridge College. She saw immediately that Cambridge Health Alliance, with its multicultural focus, could be a "gold mine" of employment opportunity for these skilled, multilingual people.

With grant support, Peterson developed a six-course, 195-hour curriculum at Cambridge College, which has a long tradition of adult education. Training covers anatomy and pathophysiology, the role of medical interpreters, interpreter skills training, and cross-cultural communication in medical interpreting. One of the most important components is a 45-hour internship at local hospitals. "That gives credibility to the program and it also gives our students availability to jobs," said Peterson. Since its inception, 120 students have matriculated into the program.

As far as Peterson is concerned, the sky's the limit. "This has made an incredible contribution to health care, and it is a gateway for bilingual immigrants to enter the medical profession in the U.S., starting with rewarding and well-paying careers in medical interpretation."

Rollins G.: Foundation for the future: Cultural competency underlies Cambridge Health Alliance language services. The Safety Net 16(1): 12–14, Spring 2002. Used with permission.

References

1. Larson L.: Is your hospital culturally competent? And what does that mean exactly? *Trustee* 58(2): 20–23, Feb. 2005.

2. Resources for Cross Cultural Health Care, the U.S. Department of Health and Human Services Office of Minority Health, and the Agency for Healthcare Research and Quality: Developing a research agenda for cultural competence in health care: Cultural competence training. *DiversityRX Home Page*, Nov. 13, 2001. www.omhrc.gov/CLAS (last accessed May 13, 2005).

3. Smedley B.D., Stith A.Y., Nelson A.R. (eds.): *Unequal Treatment: Confronting Racial and Ethnic Disparities in Health Care*. Committee on Understanding and Eliminating Racial and Ethnic Disparities in Health Care. The National Academies Press. National Academy of Sciences, 2003.

4. Betancourt J.R., et al: *Cultural Competence in Health Care: Emerging Frameworks and Practical Approaches*. The Commonwealth Fund, Oct. 2002.

5. Resources for Cross Cultural Health Care, the U.S. Department of Health and Human Services Office of Minority Health, and the Agency for Healthcare Research and Quality: Cultural competency of health professionals. *DiversityRX Home Page*, Nov. 13, 2001. www.DiversityRx.org/best/1_6.htm#161 (last accessed May 13, 2005).

6. Health Resources and Services Administration, U.S. Department of Health and Human Services: Cultural Competence Works: Using cultural competence to improve the quality of health care for diverse populations and add value to managed care arrangements. 2001.

7. Rollins G.: Diversity Training; Finding ways to sustain resource-intensive efforts. *The Safety Net* pp. 11–12, Fall 2003.

8. Thompson-Robinson M., Cornelius D.: An Overview and Evaluation of Cultural Competence Training for Public Health Professionals. *Florida Public Health Review* 1:16–23, 2004.

9. Cross Cultural Health Care Program (CCHCP): Training programs. *Cross Cultural Health Care Program (CCHCP) Home Page*. www.xculture.org/training/overview/interpreter/ (last accessed May 11, 2005).

10. Grantmakers in Health: In the right words: Addressing language and culture in providing health care. Issue brief no. 18, Aug. 2003.

11. National Council on Interpreting in Health Care (NCIHC): Models for the Provision of Health Care Interpreter Training. *NCIHC Home Page*, Feb. 2002. www.ncihc.org/NCIHC_PDF/Training.pdf (last accessed May 13, 2005).

12. Resources for Cross Cultural Health Care, the U.S. Department of Health and Human Services Office of Minority Health, and the Agency for Healthcare Research and Quality: Culturally competent health services. *DiversityRx Home Page*, Nov. 13, 2001. www.DiversityRx.org/best/1_3.htm#131 (last accessed May 11, 2005).

Five

The Business Case
for Cultural
and Linguistic
Competence

American health policy is focused on quality as never before. In legislation, regulation, enforcement, policy development, and market demands, many initiatives are under way to improve the quality of health care in the United States.[1]

This chapter looks at how these forces of change have affected the emergence of cultural competence as a viable intervention, and whether they support the case of cultural competence as a viable investment in the business of health care. In defining the business case for cultural competence, this chapter examines the incentives of achieving standards requirements, quality care, and cost effectiveness. It looks at the role of leadership in recognizing and promoting the financial rewards of cultural competence and, finally, it considers both the challenges and promise of cultural competence as a business strategy in the years ahead.

A business case exists if the investing party believes a positive indirect effect on organizational function and sustainability will occur within a reasonable time frame. This broad definition allows for a wide variety of measures to judge whether a case has been made that a particular intervention will improve both the quality and the business impact of the services at issue.

Recognizing Incentives in the Business Case for Cultural Competence

According to the 2002 report "Reducing Disparities through Culturally Competent Health Care: An Analysis of the Business Case,"[3] the business case supporting the need for health care organizations to provide cultural competence revolves around the following four interrelated financial incentives:

1. Appeal to minority consumers
2. Compete for private purchaser business
3. Respond to public purchaser demands
4. Improve cost effectiveness

Each incentive is discussed in detail below.

Appeal to Minority Consumers

The first incentive for health care organizations to become culturally competent is to increase their market share, according to the report. With minority groups accounting for 70% of the total population growth in the decade between 1988 and 1998, and the U.S. Census Bureau's projection that 4 of 10 Americans will belong to a racial or ethnic minority group by 2030, cultural competence can be an effective tool in appealing to the members of this growing market.

TIP
Because Americans are given the option to choose and change their health care plans and providers, public health organizations need to attract, retain, and satisfy multicultural populations as both employees and consumers to secure and maintain a competitive edge in the marketplace.[4]

As mentioned in Chapter One, Hispanics accounted for half the 2.9 million U.S. population growth from 2003 to 2004 and now constitute one seventh of all people in the U.S., according to a 2005 Census Bureau report. The Census Bureau estimated 41.3 million Hispanics live in the U.S. A recent article in the *Atlanta Journal-Constitution* reported an upsurge in business for Atlanta hospitals due to the high rate of births to Hispanic mothers. According to the article, Hispanic births in the state of Georgia grew by 643% in the last decade.[4] By promoting and advertising their cultural competence, health care organizations are more likely to attract the business of minority group members.

For example, at the Fifth Annual Multicultural Pharmaceutical Marketing, Media, and Public Relations meeting in March 2004, training was offered in how pharmaceutical and health care brands can "learn to build multi-level relationships with the ethnic consumer and community."[4] Articles in the provider trade press focus on the ways in which health care organizations can use cultural competence to draw in consumers looking for comfortable access and service.[3]

Sidebar 5-1.
Assessing Health Plans Through Quality Measures

The Health Plan Employers Data and Information Set (HEDIS), developed by the National Committee for Quality Assurance (NCQA), is an example of quality measures for health plans. HEDIS is intended to give purchasers and consumers a basis for comparison among health plans. Its most recent data include a few indicators of the availability of linguistically appropriate clinical and administrative services. Overall, HEDIS scores can be used to assess the quality of plans that serve a high proportion of minority enrollees.

The HEDIS data are not reported by racial and ethnic groups, and therefore the quality of care for minority enrollees cannot be separately analyzed. However, poor service to minority groups in plans that have a sizeable portion of minority enrollees would reduce those plans' overall performance in HEDIS measures.

NCQA also requires health plans to conduct the Consumer Assessment of Health Plans Survey (CAHPS) as part of HEDIS. The CAHPS core survey includes such items as satisfaction with choice of physicians and whether physicians explain things in an understandable way and show respect for what the patient has to say. The CAHPS supplemental survey asks about difficulties in communication and the availability of interpreters. CAHPS, therefore, provides additional measures of cultural competence. These measures are increasingly used by private purchasers to guide their decisions.

Source: Brach C., Fraser I.: Reducing disparities through culturally competent health care: An analysis of the business case. *Quality Management in Health Care* 10(4):15–28, 2002. Used with permission.

Compete for Private Purchaser Business

A second financial incentive for cultural competence, according to the "Reducing Disparities" report, is to improve the health care organization's performance on quality measures of interest to private purchasers, particularly in competitive markets with a large minority population. See Sidebar 5-1. Assessing Health Plans Through Quality Measures for an outline of the process.

As an example of using this quality measure, the "Reducing Disparities" report cites a group of large private purchasers that have developed a common request for information (RFI) to use in soliciting bids from health plans. This common RFI calls for not only HEDIS and CAHPS data, but also for additional information related to safety, quality, and cultural competence. To the

I P
Although purchasers face multiple competing interests (from rising health care costs and premiums to drug costs) and a lack of knowledge about the issue, many experts agree that both public and private purchasers can help facilitate cultural competence.[5]

I P

In general, experts suggest a combination of information, research, and activism to facilitate cultural competence in managed care.[6]

extent that purchasers and consumers factor in HEDIS, CAHPS, and RFI data when selecting health care organizations that serve minority populations, the report contends that culturally competent health care organizations will fare better than others.

At a 2003 meeting of the Consortium for Eliminating Health Care Disparities Through Community and Hospital Partnerships, and the National Advisory Panel, consortium member Ann Beal stated, "The major purchasers of health care are also employers of the diverse working population. If I'm New York City MTA (Metropolitan Transportation Authority), 10% of my employees are minority. Then I'm certainly going to want to have a plan that is available to my employees . . .[one] that I know will make sure that they get in to work everyday."[7]

Organizations can increase cultural competence by using the influence of health care purchasers (government and private), developing contractual requirements (federal and state), and formulating accreditation standards (for hospitals and medical schools).[6]

One initiative that could advance the process of increasing cultural competence is by incorporating culturally competent measures or health disparity indicators as part of the HEDIS. This would allow employers and purchasers to respond to evidence-based outcomes. In this case, data should reflect the clinical impact of interventions, such as reducing hospitalization, increasing satisfaction, and improving market share and member loyalty.[5]

Another initiative involves educating employees about disparities and cultural competence and empowering them to request more culturally appropriate services from the managed care provider their employer has retained.

Respond to Public Purchaser Demands

A third business incentive for culturally competent health care involves public purchasers such as Medicare and Medicaid, which are putting more emphasis on cultural competence and quality.[3]

The Centers for Medicare and Medicaid Services (CMS), the federal agency that administers the Medicare and Medicaid programs, provides the primary source for federal funding to help states and health care providers pay for language services. In 2000, CMS reminded states that they could obtain federal matching funds for language services provided to Medicaid and the State Children's Health Insurance Program (SCHIP).[5]

CMS is encouraging cultural competence in several ways. Their contracts contain culturally competent provisions

I P

Because a significant portion of health plans rely on Medicare and Medicaid business, complying with such regulations and practices is an incentive for promoting cultural competence.

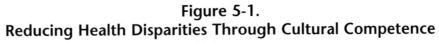

Figure 5-1.
Reducing Health Disparities Through Cultural Competence

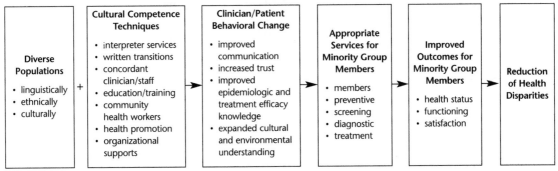

Source: Brach C., Fraser I.: Reducing disparities through culturally competent health care: An analysis of the business case. *Quality Management in Health Care* 10(4):15–28, 2002. Used with permission.

and requirements that organizations must be aware of and adhere to. Any health care organization wanting Medicare or Medicaid business must also comply with their respective regulations and purchasing practices.[5]

Figure 5-1. Reducing Health Disparities Through Cultural Competence provides an overview of the process of implementing cultural competence.

Improve Cost-Effectiveness

The fourth financial incentive for organizations to become culturally competent, according to the "Reducing Disparities Through Culturally Competent Health Care" report, is to reduce costs in caring for patients by improving cost effectiveness. Because cultural competence has the potential to change both clinicians and patient behaviors in ways that result in the provision of more appropriate services, reductions in costs can be realized in both the short and the long run.

> **T I P**
> Hiring bilingual staff or interpreters should be viewed as a cost-effective intervention when it results in more accurate medical histories that can help eliminate unnecessary testing.

Take the example of a $1.6 million federal grant that was awarded a partnership in Chicago to improve retention of nurses in the health care system. This grant was aimed at improving patient care with respect to quality, cost effectiveness, and cultural competence.[8]

The business case for cultural competence includes both incentives and limitations. Table 5-1. Incentives and Limitations in the Business Case for Cultural Competence on page 108 lists the most common of these.

Financial arrangements between plans and providers would allow plans to reap the rewards of investments in cultural competence and give providers incentives to use cultural competence techniques.[3]

Table 5-1.
Incentives and Limitations in
the Business Case for Cultural Competence

Incentives	Limitations
To increase enrollment	Fear of adverse selection
To compete for private purchaser business	Measurement difficulty
	Purchasers tendency to respond primarily to price
To respond to public purchaser's demands	Lack of definition and monitoring/enforcement
To reduce costs	Emphasis on short-term cost effectiveness
	Enrollee/patient turnover
	Inability to capture cost savings[3]

Source: Brach C., Fraser I.: Reducing disparities through culturally competent health care: An analysis of the business case. *Quality Management in Health Care* 10(4):15–28, 2002. Used with permission.

The Costs of Understanding Patient Beliefs and Practices

To ensure wise investment of what are often limited resources in achieving desired outcomes, health care organizations and professionals need to be knowledgeable of evidence-based practices that have proven to be effective in caring for specific racial, ethnic, and linguistic populations.[8]

 I P
Health organizations cannot afford—in financial as well as practical terms—to ignore the community's own strengths, expertise, and creative solutions.[8]

Research studies that include focus groups of community members often report findings about health beliefs and practices that, if unknown and unattended, might lead to costly and unnecessary interventions. Several studies have found that many African American men and women prefer to receive cancer-screening services from their own physicians instead of from screening services at clinics and health fairs.[9] Until these African American men and women were asked about their thoughts and beliefs, health care organizations knew only that their interventions and public health messages were not as effective in reaching this population.

Other studies have pointed to links between the racial and ethnic diversity of the health care workforce and health care quality. For example, studies have found that when doctor and patient share the same racial or ethnic background, patient satisfaction and self-rated quality of care are higher.[6] Higher satisfaction and self-rated care are, in turn, closely linked to certain health outcomes.

The Costs of Both Language and Communication Barriers

Language barriers between provider and patient tend to emerge in health care systems that are not responsive to the needs of diverse patient populations. Systems lacking interpreter services or culturally and linguistically appropriate health education materials lead to patient dissatisfaction, poor comprehension and adherence, and lower-quality care.[6]

The same disparities in care arise when communication barriers, apart from language barriers, erode trust between patient and provider. Trust and communication suffer when health care providers fail to understand sociocultural differences between themselves and their patients.[6]

 I P
When providers fail to take into account cultural factors—such as social status, family make up, understanding and treatment of health issues, beliefs, values, and spiritual or religious orientation—they may resort to stereotyping, which can affect their behavior and clinical decision making. These factors can contribute to services that are not cost effective.

Considering Leadership in the Business Case for Cultural Competence

Many health care executives recognize the case for integrating cultural competence into their organizational mission. The internal and external issues encouraging them to consider the effects of cultural competence include the following:

- Increasing need for primary care sites to accommodate increased volume
- Requests for better information technology to assist health professionals in caring for culturally diverse enrollees
- Greater demand for interpreters
- State and federal health plan requirements[10]

How Leaders Can Wield Influence in Implementing Cultural Competence

Leadership that makes cultural competence a priority also recognizes the changing demand from the community. By establishing priorities and targeting financial investment, the executive sets direction and creates model behavior within the health care organization and the community. CEOs build workforce and community trust by these measures.

Questions that CEOs and health care leaders must consider about their organization in assessing their cultural competence programs include the following:

- Does the program have a structure to bridge the gap between current research and implications for clinical practice for racially and ethnically diverse groups?
- Do program staff routinely survey research studies and emerging bodies of evidence?
- Does the program have a mechanism to examine research findings and their implications for policy and clinical protocols within the program?
- Does the program emphasize either contributing to or examining current research related to ethnic and racial disparities in health and quality improvement?
- Does a mechanism exist to keep abreast of new developments in pharmacology, particularly as they relate to racially and ethnically diverse groups?
- Does the program have a systematic approach to provide evidence-based or best-practice interventions that have proven efficacy for specific racial and ethnic populations?
- Does a forum exist to share research findings and interests related to racial and ethnic disparities in health?
- Are incentives and grant support available to pursue or contribute to research on racial and ethnic health disparities?[11]

 I P

Organization leaders possess a significant level of influence. Even their simple actions—such as formally scheduling cultural competence meetings and discussions and participating in the training direct patient care providers receive—can have an impact on their organization. More concrete actions, such as conducting cultural competence reviews, can increase the visibility of the issue within the organization and can lead to the involvement of individuals who otherwise may go unheard.

CEOs should be aware that initiatives and actions vary greatly and depend in large measure on patient needs, communities being served, type of health care organization, workforce, and other factors. Such strategies, however, are likely to include several common points, including the following:

- Educating and involving the board of trustees
- Conducting a review or assessment to identify current strengths and challenges
- Introducing cultural competency into contracts and operations
- Using culturally competent hiring and workforce actions

- Integrating cultural competence into management and line staff meetings
- Building diversity accountability into staff hiring, promotion, and staff support actions
- Designating a specific cultural competence skill as part of position descriptions
- Conducting diversity training for all staff,[12] regularly evaluating the training program, updating its content, and monitoring its impact into daily practices.[11]

How Leaders Can Establish the Principles of Cultural Competence

The nation's health care systems and health policies are shaped by the leaders who design them and the workforce that carries them out. It is the leaders of health care organizations who set the framework for defining cultural competence and implementing culturally competent practices. Understanding the principles of organizational cultural competence, systemic cultural competence, and clinical cultural competence is key to the effectiveness of those practices.

Recommendations to achieve organizational cultural competence focus on promoting minorities into positions of leadership in health care and recruiting minorities into the health professions. Systemic cultural competence recommendations focus on eliminating systemic or institutional barriers to care and improving the health care system's ability to monitor and improve the quality of care. Clinical cultural competence recommendations center on enhancing health professionals' awareness of cultural issues and health beliefs while providing methods to elicit, negotiate, and manage this information after it is obtained. Sidebar 5-2. Recommendations to Achieve Organizational Cultural Competence, Systemic Cultural Competence, and Clinical Cultural Competence on pages 112 and 113 expands on these recommendations.

Recognizing Tools for the Business Case

Experts have drawn clear links among cultural competence, quality improvement, and the elimination of racial or ethnic disparities in care. Although acknowledging many causes for such disparities, efforts to improve quality through greater cultural competence at multiple levels are especially important.

Although emphasizing the importance of racial and ethnic diversity in health care leadership and the health care workforce, as well as stressing the benefits of involving community members in the health care process, experts suggest using tools and benchmarks to evaluate outcomes—creating a standard of care for evaluation of care. They also identify a need to translate cultural competence into quality indi-

> *T I P*
> Culturally competent adjustments in health care delivery can further the quality improvement movement as a whole and should occur at the systemic and clinical encounter levels.[5]

Sidebar 5-2. Recommendations to Achieve Organizational Cultural Competence, Systemic Cultural Competence, and Clinical Cultural Competence

Organizational cultural competence

- Programs that advance minority health care leadership should be encouraged and existing programs should be strengthened to develop a cadre of professionals who may assume influential positions in academia, government, and private industry.
- Organizations should make it a priority to hire and promote minorities in the health care workforce.
- Community representatives should be formally or informally involved in the health care organization's planning and quality improvement meetings, whether as part of the board or as part of focus groups, for example.

Systemic cultural competence

- On-site interpreters should be available in health care settings where a significant proportion of patients has limited English proficiency (LEP); for example, more than 15%. Other types of interpreter services, such as remote telephone or simultaneous interpretation, should be used in settings with fewer LEP patients or with limited financial or human resources.
- Key health information should reflect the appropriate level of health literacy, language proficiency, and cultural norms for the populations being served. This includes signage, specific programs for health promotion and disease prevention, health education materials, pre- and post-procedure instructions, informed-consent forms, and advanced directives, among other materials.
- Large health care purchasers, both private and public, should require systemic cultural competence interventions (such as racial and ethnic data collection or interpreter services) as part of their contracting language.
- Organizations should identify federal and state reimbursement strategies for interpreter services.
- The federal government should enforce Title VI requirements mandating the provision of interpreter services in health care settings. Institutions should be held accountable for substandard services.
- Researchers should identify tools to detect medical errors that result from lack of systemic cultural competence, including those stemming from language barriers (such as taking a prescribed medication incorrectly); misunderstanding health education materials, instructions, or

signage (such as inappropriately preparing for a diagnostic or therapeutic procedure, resulting in postponement or delay); and misunderstanding the benefits and risks of procedures requiring informed consent.

- The Joint Commission and the NCQA should incorporate standards for measuring systemic cultural competence.
- Government programs (such as Medicare and Medicaid), recipients of federal funding (such as hospitals), and private organizations (such as managed care plans) should collect data on race, ethnicity, and language preference for all beneficiaries, members, and clinical encounters to facilitate monitoring disparities, reporting quality data, and implementing initiatives to improve care.

Clinical cultural competence

- Cross-cultural training should be a required, integrated component of the training and professional development of health care providers at all levels. The curricula should increase awareness of racial and ethnic disparities in health and the importance of sociocultural factors on health beliefs and behaviors; identify the impact of race, ethnicity, culture, and class on clinical decision making; develop tools to assess the community members' health beliefs and behaviors; and develop human resource skills for cross-cultural assessment, communication, and negotiation.
- Quality improvement efforts should include culturally and linguistically appropriate patient survey methods as well as process and outcome measures that reflect the needs of multicultural and minority populations.
- Programs should be developed to help patients understand and navigate the health care system and become a more active partner in the clinical encounter.

Source: Betancourt J.R., et al: *Cultural Competence in Health Care: Emerging Frameworks and Practical Approaches*. The Commonwealth Fund, Oct. 2002. Used with permission.

cators or outcomes that can be measured. Not only is this standard of evaluation of care recommended as a tool with which to eliminate barriers and disparities, but as a set of measuring points that will make the business case for cultural competence.[7] After all, in making the business case for cultural competence, CEOs and other health care leaders should always be mindful that effective cultural competence practices could lead to advancements in diagnosis.

Case Study 5-1. Leadership Support, Training, and Collaboration as an Investment in Cultural Competence at Rowan Regional Medical Center on pages 114–117 is one example of a North Carolina medical center whose leaders examined the business case, conducted an internal assessment, and implemented a team approach in increasing cultural competence organizationwide.

*C*ASE STUDY 5.1
Leadership Support, Training, and Collaboration as an Investment in Cultural Competence at Rowan Regional Medical Center

The historic city of Salisbury, North Carolina, with a population of 130,340, is the county seat of Rowan County and is the home of Rowan Regional Medical Center (RRMC). Rowan County populations served per statistical data include White 80%, African American 15.8%, American Indian and Alaskan native 0.3%, Asian 0.8%, Native Hawaiian and other Pacific Islander 0.0%, Hispanic or Latin American 5.1%.

The facility is a private, nonprofit, short term acute care organization composed of a 308-bed capacity, rendering services in maternity, cardiology, oncology, inpatient rehabilitation, outpatient services, 24-hour emergency services, outpatient drug/chemical dependency services, inpatient psychiatric services, home health, and hospice.

Addressing the Issue

RRMC began dialogue to address an ongoing global issue with state and regional hospital administrators, associations, and Area Health Education Center (AHEC) organizations. Those associations partnered to communicate the nursing shortage dilemma in the following campaigns: The Commonwealth Fund publication entitled "Cultural Competence in Health Care," The American Hospital Association's Commission on Workforce report entitled "In Our Hands: How Hospital Leaders Can Build a Thriving Workforce," The North Carolina Center for Nursing's marketing "toolkit" for recruitment, AHEC summer camps, and other marketing resources depicting diversity to raise awareness of health careers among men and underrepresented minorities.

Gaining Leadership Support

With the ongoing global issue of the nursing shortage and the prevalence of local aging nurses in the organization, the challenge of workforce retention and the movement of an increased multicultural community and workforce are the key issues that sparked the flame of interest in leadership at RRMC to acknowledge, investigate, and support interventional measures that challenge the provision of quality, culturally and linguistically competent health care. These key issues also raised the awareness of leadership to look at the business case of diversity for turning visions into reality and to maintain a competitive edge. These findings set the precedence for RRMC to identify tangible methods of addressing health care recruitment in underrepresented populations and workforce retention strategies, and raise the organization's cultural consciousness, awareness, knowledge, and skills about differences that exist.

The initial starting point was the key to implementing this initiative. To start, presentations regarding hospital employee training, recruitment efforts, retention efforts, community outreach, and awareness promotions were presented to the hospital board of directors and approved.

Seeking Collaboration

RRMC's VP of patient care services, Claire Wilkie, R.N., M.P.H., M.H.A., collaborated with three other local regional hospitals to write a grant proposal to the Duke Endowment Healthcare Division. The Duke Endowment awarded an appropriation in the amount of $1.3 million to assist in carrying out the grant objectives—outlined in a summary plan titled "Enhancing the Diversity of Health Professionals in Community Hospitals in North Carolina"—for programs to be implemented in the four hospitals beginning May 2003 through May 2006. Yvonne W. Dixon, R.N., B.S.N., was the candidate chosen for the position as Rowan Regional Medical Center Diversity Health Careers Coordinator.

Developing a Baseline Assessment

In meeting the initial objectives of the grant, all grant recipient hospitals chose the same diversity consulting firm to obtain a baseline cultural assessment of the organizations. Empirical data collected from RRMC was based on the interviews of the executive level and three focus groups consisting of department directors, multidiscipline, and nursing.

The findings of the assessment demonstrated that a multicultural health care organization could suffer from problems such as stereotyping, prejudicing, difficulty in communicating, predicting behavior, and built-in discriminatory processes. The main result of the assessment clearly addressed:

- The benefits of culturally enhancing leadership organizationwide
- Perfecting workforce cultural problem-solving techniques
- Improving organizational flexibility and accountability
- Acknowledging workforce satisfaction, productivity, effectiveness, and efficiency
- Increasing customer relations and satisfaction
- Seeing an increase in business profits

Furthermore, the findings strongly suggested implementing organizationwide diversity training and genuine partnerships with community and civic groups to enhance the organization's development of increased community trust, social image, and cultural communication competency skills.

Taking Action

From this point, the journey to cultural and linguistic competency for RRMC began by attempting to create a positive climate that supports diversity, which is strongly related to the presence of organizational, job, and career attitudes. The environment will become more productive when employees feel valued and their talents are fully utilized.

Additionally, an increased diverse population of customers will feel more comfortable in using the health care facility and the initiative will contribute to the organization's overall success.

Creating a Cultural Competence Committee

The organization resurrected the Cultural Diversity Task Force and, by improving its visibility, mission, and accountability, renamed the group the Cultural Diversity Customer First Council. New representatives were appointed, including physicians and employees from multidiscipline departments. The council representatives meet every second Friday to discuss organizational diversity issues and best practices, implement the provision for employee diversity educational learning tools, and address issues for organizational improvement and support.

Training the Staff

From this group, six diversity trainers were selected to participate in a train-the-trainer course—made up of four-hour days—the diversity consultant firm provided. After the train-the-trainer sessions were completed, the trainer representatives and coordinator presented a proposal recommendation for employee training to the executive administrators of RRMC. The employee training objectives were intentionally executed for simplicity, employee transitional ease, and instilling trust in the initiative in which every employee is required to participate.

The proposal was approved, and organizationwide four-hour cultural diversity training sessions began in May 2004 and were completed in July 2005 for existing employees. Additionally, a two-hour training for the new employee orientation was approved and began implementation in July 2005.

Considering Measurement Outcomes

Embracing diversity requires an investment of time, focus, and people who are accountable for long-term objectives. Measuring results will take a long time. The most important goal in managing this initiative is to create a safe, accepting, innovative, and respectful workplace, which acknowledges and removes barriers that maintain, reinforce, and impede growth. Since the inception of this diversity initiative, multicultural recruitment efforts have increased, AHEC library resources have increased, Spanish classes are offered to employees, presentations to middle and high school students interested in health careers have increased, programs targeting high school students for internships and job shadowing experiences are ongoing, collaborative efforts with universities and colleges to partner for clinical curriculums have increased, awareness promotions are ongoing, partnering with the City of Salisbury and community civic organizations' diversity efforts are ongoing, educational presentations have been provided to the medical staff, and the Nursing Recognition, Recruitment, and Retention Council has restructured to address current cultural practices.

There is, however, room for a great deal of improvement related to interpersonal and subgroup communication. Miscommunication can create misunderstandings—which leads to conflict—and pose barriers to cooperation. Now, more than ever before at RRMC, these issues are being acknowledged, identified, and addressed.

 I P
Change relies on teamwork. If any member of the team is not willing to engage in creative problem solving, the number of ways to achieve the goal is limited. A consistent communication process that keeps members informed, involved, and inspired should be built into any strategy that provokes positive change in practice or environment.[13]

In making the business case for cultural competence, health care organizations must, again, rely on and collaborate with the communities they serve. Measuring the performance of cultural competence programming involves a consistent and comprehensive structure of data collection and analysis that can only be achieved through the contributions of an organization's patient population.

The two most essential issues to consider before an organization can move forward with a critical assessment of its cultural competence programming involve team leadership and a collective belief in the overarching goals of the process.

Without a team approach to leadership, organizations are unable to achieve cultural competence. It takes understanding, commitment, and persistence on the part of staff, board members, and volunteers. And, organizations cannot achieve cultural competence without everyone firmly believing that becoming a diverse organization is as important as any other goal in the program's strategic plan.[13] It is common for an organization to experience varying levels of belief in new programming at its outset, but any resistance to the process from board members or staff must be overcome before programming can be adequately measured.

As the chapters of this book have illustrated, establishing cultural competence involves much more than putting into place simple action strategies that will at some point be evaluated by leadership. Initiating cultural competence practices requires that an organization examine all aspects of its programming—its mission and goals; staff and leadership composition; policies and practices; nomination, election, and hiring practices; its public relations and recruitment plan; training; volunteer management practices; and even its physical facility—to determine the steps that need to be taken to improve the safe provision of quality health care for all.

References

1. Gosfield A.G.: *Doing Well By Doing Good: Improving the Business Case for Quality*. Philadelphia: Alice G. Gosfield and Associates, P.C., 2003.

2. Leatherman S., Berwick D.: The business case for quality: Case studies and an analysis. *Health Affairs* 22(2):17, Mar. 2003.

3. Brach C., Fraser I.: Reducing disparities through culturally competent health care: An analysis of the business case. *Quality Management in Health Care* 10(4):15–28, 2002.

4. Health Research and Educational Trust (HRET): Eliminating disparities through community and hospital partnerships: Summary of the national panel advisory meeting, Nov. 5, 2003, *Health Research and Educational Trust (HRET) Home Page*. www.aha.org/hret/programs/eliminatingdisparities.html (last accessed May 10, 2005).

5. Grantmakers in Health: In the right words: Addressing language and culture in providing health care. Issue brief no. 18: Aug. 2003.

6. Betancourt J.R., et al: *Cultural Competence in Health Care: Emerging Frameworks and Practical Approaches*. The Commonwealth Fund, Oct. 2002.

7. Health Research and Educational Trust (HRET): A toolkit for collecting race, ethnicity, and primary language information from patients. *Health Research and Educational Trust (HRET) Home Page*. www.hretdisparities.org/hretdisparities/index.jsp (last accessed May 11, 2005).

8. National Center for Cultural Competence (NCCC): Public health in a multicultural environment. *National Center for Cultural Competence (NCCC) Home Page*. www.nccccurricula.info/public/C9.html (last accessed May 11, 2005).

9. Institute of Medicine (IOM): Crossing the Quality Chasm. Washington D.C.: The National Academy Press, 2001.

10. Adapted from Grantmakers in Health: In the right words: Addressing language and culture in providing health care. Issue brief no. 18: Aug. 2003.

11. Goode T.: Implications of cultural and linguistic competence for evidence-based practice: Public health in a multicultural environment (Appendix A). *National Center for Cultural Competence Home Page*, 2004. www.nccccurricula.info/resources_mod4.html (last accessed May 13, 2005).

12. Second national conference on quality health care for culturally diverse populations: Strategy and action for communities, providers, and a changing health system, Oct. 11–14, 2000. *DiversityRX Home Page*. www.diversityrx.org/CCCONF/00/00_proc_03.htm#A (last accessed May 10, 2005).

13. National Court Appointed Special Advocate (CASA): Cultural competence in your program. *CASANet Home Page*. www.casanet.org/program-management/diversity/cultural-competence.htm (last accessed May 10, 2005).

Appendix A

An Overview and Evaluation of Cultural Competence Training for Public Health Professionals

Phase I of Project: Development of Training Curriculum

The first phase of this project was the development of a training curriculum and materials. The Institute of Public Health was responsible for this development. The training curriculum covered six modules as follows:

Module 1: Introduction and Pre-Assessment

In this module, the pre-assessment tool assessed participants' knowledge, attitudes, and self-efficacy to the provision of culturally competent services.

Module 2: Culture and Its Influence on Health

The purpose of this module was to define culture and related terms, and discuss the relevance of culture to health.

Module 3: Cultural Competence

This module defined cultural competence as the desire, skills, and knowledge necessary to enable organizations, systems, and individual providers to work effectively and provide services consistent with the cultural context of the client.

Module 4: Conceptual Framework for the Provision of Culturally Competent Services in Public Health Settings

In this module, the conceptual framework for the provision of culturally competent services in public health settings was reviewed and discussed.

Module 5: Application of Cultural Competence

For this module, participants applied the newly learned concepts to their own circumstance by participating in a group activity.

Module 6: Conclusion and Post-Assessment

Finally, in this module participants completed appropriate evaluation forms.

Each training session lasted for one full eight-hour day. These sessions had a didactic as well as an experiential component. The Conceptual Framework for the Provision of Culturally Competent Services in Public Health Settings was the basis on which the training curriculum was developed. The Conceptual Framework for the Provision of Culturally Competent Services in Public Health Settings is an ecological approach that incorporates contextual elements as well as the service delivery system and clients in the provision of culturally competent services. This framework describes how the service delivery system, client, and contextual elements interact in providing culturally competent services in public health settings. Included in this description are characteristics, which facilitate and optimize these interactions.

Phase II of Project: Implementation of Training Curriculum

The second phase of the project implemented the training curriculum. Trainings were held in six sites throughout Florida during a six week period. The sites for the trainings were identified by the Florida Department of Health.

Phase III of Project: Evaluation

The third phase of the project was an ongoing evaluation of the training program. This evaluation occurred at the process and impact levels. The process evaluation examined the training program's fidelity to the developed curriculum as well as the quality of the curriculum and training. The impact, or short-term, evaluation was conducted to determine whether changes occurred in participants' knowledge, attitudes, and beliefs regarding cultural competence and its incorporation into service provision.

Methods of Process Evaluation

Multiple methods were used for the process evaluation. In terms of monitoring the implementation of the trainings, tracking the registrations for each session and debriefings between the Institute of Public Health and Office of Equal Opportunity and Minority staffs were done. Each person wanting to participate in the training session was asked to complete a registration form and demographic sheet, and data from these forms were used for further analysis.

Informal debriefings were completed to gather the impressions of project staff after each training session. Based on these debriefings, minor alterations were made to the training session to enhance the learning experience for all participants.

A session evaluation form was developed to monitor the perceptions of the participants. This evaluation form asked participants to rate the quality of the session, content, and instruction. This form was distributed to all participants at the end of each training session. A content analysis, looking for themes, was performed with the qualitative data from the comment section of these forms.

Methods for Impact Evaluation

The impact evaluation focused on whether observable changes occurred in participants' knowledge, attitudes, and beliefs based on the training session. This change was assessed through the administration of a pre-assessment at the beginning and post-assessment at the end of each training session. The questions on these assessment forms were divided into two sections. The first section examined knowledge, attitudes, and beliefs related to the provision of culturally competent services. Response categories for most items were 1=Strongly Agree, 2=Just Agree, 3=Just Disagree, and 4=Strongly Disagree. For these items, a higher score was deemed better. For those items marked (***), the response categories were reversed: 1=Strongly Disagree, 2=Disagree, 3=Just Agree, 4=Strongly Agree. A lower score for the item was deemed better.

The second section inquired about the participants' ability to meet each of the objectives of the training session. All data from the assessments were collected for analysis.

Participants also completed a "Contract with Myself." This form asked participants to comment on the information learned through participating in the training; how they planned to use the information in daily work activities; skills and knowledge needed in cultural competence; and other activities they planned to undertake to enhance their knowledge of cultural competence in the future.

Results of Process Evaluation. One hundred sixty-six (166) participants attended a training session at one of the six training sites.

Based on the responses on the session evaluation forms, participants found the content appropriate, the trainer to be effective, and they learned about cultural competence. Regarding the content analysis of the comment section of the evaluation form, those participants who responded indicated that they liked the trainer and the training. These participants also felt that this training should be offered in such a way that more people from their work unit could attend.

One hundred twenty-seven (127) participants in the training completed and returned the "Contract with Myself." Based on the content analysis of "Contract with Myself," major themes emerged for each of the items participants were asked to respond to. For the first item, "The key point(s) that I learned in Cultural Competence Training: Eliminating Racial and Ethnic Health Disparities in Florida is/are," two themes emerged due to a high response frequency. The first theme was about understanding culture and its importance, other cultural terms, and cultural competence. Most participants indicated that they did not know how culture, race, and ethnicity were defined. Participants indicated learning that "culture is very important in the provision of services and how they are received." A second theme emerged as participants also realized that "there are many diverse points involved in cultural competence that must be taken into perspective in order to deliver services that are culturally appropriate," and that "cultural competence is more than just being aware of different cultures."

Increasing organizational awareness was also one of the most important points that participants learned through the training. Participants felt that "to increase organizational awareness of the hiring of personnel who are sensitive to and aware of cultural competence" would be beneficial in reducing health disparities in the state of Florida.

Participants felt that if their organization could learn "how to incorporate diverse cultures into our mission/values statements and make sure all employees have an intent to carry out the mission," it would help implement cultural competence among their employees.

In response to "When I return to my work unit, I plan to use this information in my daily activities to/by," numerous participants stated that they would use the information learned at the training in their daily activities by educating other staff, listening to and communicating with the clients, focusing on issues specific to all cultures, incorporating cultural competence into their services, and improving their own knowledge. Almost half of the respondents felt that educating their organization as well as other staff members would aid in developing skills in the area of cultural competence.

Many participants indicated that they plan to listen to and communicate with their clients. Participants also felt that being "more sensitive and using a focus group to find out what the target group wants" will add to the overall goal of ensuring cultural competence. This information will also be used by "putting more attention on the individual and the different groups and learning" more about the clients' culture and by "asking more questions of clients about their culture, customs, beliefs, values, etc. rather than assuming I know" about the client based on their feedback.

For the next item, "To be more culturally competent, I need to develop more skills in the area of," participants identified a variety of skills and knowledge areas that included culture of clients, language, and listening/communication. More than half the participants felt that finding out more information about the clients' culture is extremely beneficial to providing culturally competent services.

Listening and communicating skills were also identified as aiding in the application of culturally competent services. For example, one participant indicated a skill to "become a better listener." Many participants saw ways to improve their skills by "listening to others rather than forming an opinion" as well as "listening and allowing others to voice their opinions, even if I don't agree." Finally, participants responded to "I plan to further develop my cultural competence skills by...". More than half the participants felt that education, implementing cultural competence, and involving the community are ways for them to further develop their cultural competence skills. Most felt education is the key to developing cultural competence skills. Some participants expressed the desire to "attend more trainings and try to learn a different language in the near future" to develop skills. Other participants will "research the subject to better understand my need to learn more about cultural issues to better help those targeted."

Some participants will "emphasize the importance of cultural competence to others and continue to educate myself." Participants viewed community involvement as a necessity for the correct functioning of cultural competence. For example, one participant indicated his or her cultural competence skills would be developed through increasing outreach efforts in communities and identifying groups to work with in the community of different cultures.

Source: Thompson-Robinson M., Cornelius D.: An Overview and Evaluation of Cultural Competence Training for Public Health Professionals. *Florida Public Health Review* 1:16–23, 2004 (Web site http://publichealth.usf.edu/fphr). Permission to use obtained from Dr. Robert J. McDermott, Editor-in-Chief, Florida Public Health Review, June 29, 2005.

Appendix B

Joint Commission's Requirement
for Collection of Information
on Language and
Communication Needs

The Joint Commission has contributed to the issue of cultural competence in health care by developing standards and elements of performance (EPs) that are related to the provision of culturally and linguistically appropriate services in the various accreditation settings—Hospital (HAP), Ambulatory (AMB), Long Term Care (LTC), Behavioral Health (BHC), and Home Care (OME). Some of the standards, listed below, directly address issues related to culturally and linguistically appropriate service provision, while other standards serve as organizational supports for such care.

Effective January 1, 2006, a new requirement for the collection of information on language and communication needs will apply to ambulatory care, behavioral health care, critical access hospital, home care, hospital, and long term care.

Standard IM.6.20

Records contain client/patient/resident-specific information, as appropriate to the care, treatment, and services provided.

Elements of Performance for IM.6.20

(Medical records) contain, as applicable, the following demographic information:

- **[Ambulatory Care]** Patient's name, gender, address, phone number, date of birth, height and weight, and the name and phone number of any legally authorized representative
- **[Behavioral Health Care]** Client's name, address, date of birth, sex, race or ethnic origin, next of kin, education, marital status, employment, and the name and phone number of any legally authorized representative
- **[Critical Access Hospital and Hospital]** Patient's name, sex, address, date of birth, and authorized representative
- **[Long Term Care]** Resident's name, address, date of birth, religion, marital status, social security number, gender, and the name of any legally authorized representative
- **[Ambulatory Care, Critical Access Hospital, and Hospital]** Legal status of patients receiving behavioral health care services
- **[Behavioral Health Care]** Legal status of clients

- **[Long Term Care]** Resident's legal status
- **[Ambulatory Care, Behavioral Health Care, Critical Access Hospital, Hospital, and Long Term Care]** The [client/patient/resident]'s language and communication needs
- **[Home Care]** The following clinical information is included in the patient record:
  - Specific notes on the care, treatment, and services
  - Assessments relevant to the care, treatment, and services
  - Authenticated, legible, and complete physician's orders, as required by law or regulation
  - Patient's relevant medical history
  - Information required by the organization's policy or law or regulation
  - The patient's language and communication needs

Glossary

abuse   Intentional maltreatment of an individual which may cause injury, either physical or psychological. *See also* neglect.

>   **mental abuse**   Includes humiliation, harassment, and threats of punishment or deprivation.

>   **physical abuse**   Includes hitting, slapping, pinching, or kicking. Also includes controlling behavior through corporal punishment.

>   **sexual abuse**   Includes sexual harassment, sexual coercion, and sexual assault.

activity services   Structured activities designed to help an individual develop or maintain creative, physical, and social skills through participation in recreation, art, dance, drama, social, or other activities.

administration   The fiscal and general management of an organization, as distinct from the direct provision of services.

administrative/financial measures   Measures that address the organizational structure for coordinating and integrating services, functions, or activities across operational components, including financial management (for example, financial stability, utilization/length of stay, credentialing).

advance directive   A document or documentation allowing a person to give directions about future medical care or to designate another person(s) to make medical decisions if the individual loses decision-making capacity. Advance directives may include living wills, durable powers of attorney, do-not-resuscitate (DNRs) orders, right to die, or similar documents listed in the Patient Self-Determination Act, which express the patient's preferences.

advanced practice nurse   A registered nurse who has gained additional knowledge and skills through successful completion of an organized program of nursing education that prepares nurses for advanced practice roles and has been certified by the Board of Nursing to engage in the practice of advanced practice nursing.

advocate   A person who represents the rights and interests of another individual as though they were the person's own, in order to realize the rights to which the individual is entitled, obtain needed services, and remove barriers to meeting the individual's needs.

behavior management and treatment   The use of basic behavioral or learning-based techniques designed to help the patient develop socially appropriate and safe replacement behavior. Characteristics of a behavior management and treatment program are that all the direct care staff are trained in the application of the program; it is a written, planned program; it is applied at all times the patient is under the supervision of direct care staff; it is individualized; and it is distinct from routine interactions with the patient.

behavioral health   A broad array of mental health, chemical dependency, habilitation, and re-habilitation services provided in settings such as inpatient, residential, and outpatient.

business case   A situation that exists for a health care improvement intervention if the entity that invests in the intervention realizes a financial return on its investment in a reasonable time frame, using a reasonable rate of discounting. This may be realized as "bankable dollars" [profit], a reduction in losses for a given program or population, or avoided costs.

care   Requires that patients and their families are treated as human beings that have lives beyond the hospital and meaning beyond the medical world of diagnoses, medications, treatment, and prognosis.

care plan   A written plan, based on data gathered during assessment, that identifies care needs, describes the strategy for providing services to meet those needs, documents treatment goals and objectives, outlines the criteria for terminating specified interventions, and documents the progress in meeting goals and objectives. The format of the plan in some organizations may be guided by patient-specific policies and procedures, protocols, practice guidelines, clinical paths, care maps, or a combination thereof. The care plan may include care, treatment, habilitation, and rehabilitation.

care planning (or planning of care)   Individualized planning and provision of services that addresses the needs, safety, and well-being of the patient. The plan, which formulates strategies, goals, and objectives, may include narratives, policies and procedures, protocols, practice guidelines, clinical paths, care maps, or a combination of these.

community   The individuals, families, groups, agencies, facilities, or institutions within the geographic area served by a health care organization.

community health workers (CHWs)   Typically members of a particular community tasked with improving the health of that community in cooperation with the health care system or public health agencies.

competence or competency   A determination of an individual's skills, knowledge, and capability to meet defined expectations.

confidentiality   An individual's right, within the law, to personal and informational privacy, including his or her health care records.

continuing care   Care provided over time; in various settings, programs, or services; spanning the illness-to-wellness continuum.

continuing education   Education beyond initial professional preparation that is relevant to the type of care delivered in an organization, that provides current knowledge relevant to an individual's field of practice or service responsibilities, and that may be related to findings from performance improvement activities.

continuity   The degree to which the care of individuals is coordinated among practitioners, among organizations, and over time.

continuum of care   Matching the individual's ongoing needs with the appropriate level and type of care, treatment, and service within an organization or across multiple organizations.

coordination of care   The process of coordinating care, treatment, and services provided by a health care organization, including referral to appropriate community resources and liaison with others (such as the individual's physician, other health care organizations, or community services involved in care, treatment, and services) to meet the ongoing identified needs of individuals, to ensure implementation of the plan of care, and to avoid unnecessary duplication of services.

cross-cultural or cultural competence training A vast array of educational activities aimed at enhancing the capacity of the service delivery system to meet the needs of different racial and ethnic populations.

culture The thoughts, communications, actions, customs, beliefs, values, and institutions of racial, ethnic, religious, or social groups.

cultural and linguistic competence The ability of health care providers and institutions to deliver effective services to racially, ethnically, and culturally diverse patient populations.

cultural embeddedness A measure of how aligned a patient is with his or her native culture.

discharge The point at which an individual's active involvement with an organization or program is terminated and the organization or program no longer maintains active responsibility for the care of the individual.

discharge planning A formalized process in a health care organization through which the need for a program of continuing and follow-up care is ascertained and, if warranted, initiated for each patient.

emergency **1.** An unexpected or sudden occasion, as in emergency surgery needed to prevent death or serious disability. **2.** A natural or man-made event that significantly disrupts the environment of care (for example, damage to the organization's building(s) and grounds due to severe winds, storms, or earthquakes); that significantly disrupts care and treatment (for example, loss of utilities such as power, water, or telephones due to floods, civil disturbances, accidents, or emergencies in the organization or its community); or that results in sudden, significantly changed or increased demands for the organization's services (for example, bioterrorist attack, building collapse, or plane crash in the organization's community). Some emergencies are called "disasters" or "potential injury creating events" (PICEs).

emergency management plan The organization's written document describing the process it would implement for managing the consequences of natural disasters or other emergencies that could disrupt the organization's ability to provide care, treatment, and services. The plan identifies specific procedures that describe mitigation, preparedness, response, and recovery strategies, actions, and responsibilities.

entry The process by which an individual comes into a setting, including screening and/or assessment by the organization or the practitioner in order to determine the capacity of the organization or practitioner to provide the care, treatment, and services required to meet the individual's needs.

family The person(s) who plays a significant role in an individual's life. This may include a person(s) not legally related to the individual. This person(s) is often referred to as a surrogate decision maker if authorized to make care decisions for the individual should he or she lose decision-making capacity.

governance The individual(s), group, or agency that has ultimate authority and responsibility for establishing policy, maintaining quality of care, and providing for organization management and planning. Other names for this group include the board, board of trustees, board of governors, and board of commissioners.

guardian A parent, trustee, conservator, committee, or other individual or agency empowered by law to act on behalf of or be responsible for an individual.

health disparity *(as defined by the Health Resources and Service Administration [HRSA])* A population-specific difference in the presence of disease, health outcomes, or access to care. Language barriers between patients and health care providers may affect all three outcomes (that is, disease incidence, health outcomes, access to care).

health literacy   The degree to which people have the capacity to obtain, process, and understand basic health information and services needed to make appropriate health decisions.

health promotion   The process by which individuals, communities, and populations are given the tools necessary to improve health outcomes.

informed consent   Agreement or permission accompanied by full notice about what is being consented to. A patient must be apprised of the nature, risks, and alternatives of a medical procedure or treatment before the physician or other health care professional begins any such course. After receiving this information, the patient then either consents to or refuses such a procedure or treatment.

leader   An individual who sets expectations, develops plans, and implements procedures to assess and improve the quality of the organization's governance, management, clinical, and support functions and processes. The leaders described in the leadership function include at least the leaders of the governing body; the chief executive officer and other senior managers; departmental leaders; the elected and the appointed leaders of the medical staff and the clinical departments and other medical staff members in organizational administrative positions; and the nurse executive and other senior nursing leaders.

limited English proficiency (LEP)   Describes persons who have difficulty speaking, reading, writing, or understanding the English language because they are individuals who

- were not born in the United States or whose primary language is a language other than English; or
- come from environments where a language other than English is dominant; or
- are American Indian and Alaskan Natives and who come from environments where a language other than English has had a significant impact on their level of English language proficiency; and
- by reason, thereof, are denied the opportunity to learn successfully in classrooms where the language of instruction is English or to participate fully in American society.

medical history   A component of the medical record consisting of an account of an individual's history, obtained whenever possible from the individual, and including at least the following information: chief complaint, details of the present illness or care needs, relevant past history, and relevant inventory by body systems.

medical interpretation   The ability to interpret the spoken conversation between provider and client within the medical context, with a specific emphasis on the ability to use and explain medical terms in both languages.

medication   Any prescription medications; sample medications; herbal remedies; vitamins; nutriceuticals; over-the-counter drugs; vaccines; diagnostic and contrast agents used on or administered to persons to diagnose, treat, or prevent disease or other abnormal conditions; radioactive medications; respiratory therapy treatments; parenteral nutrition; blood derivatives; intravenous solutions (plain, with electrolytes and/or drugs); and any product designated by the Food and Drug Administration (FDA) as a drug. This definition of medication does not include enteral nutrition solutions (which are considered food products), oxygen, and other medical gases.

medication history   A delineation of the drugs used by an individual (both past and present), including prescribed and unprescribed drugs and alcohol, along with any unusual reactions to those drugs.

mission statement   A written expression that sets forth the purpose of an organization or one of its components. The generation of a mission statement usually precedes the formation of goals and objectives.

neglect   The absence of minimal services or resources to meet basic needs. Neglect includes withholding or inadequately providing food and hydration (without physician, patient, or surrogate approval), clothing, medical care, and good hygiene. It may also include placing the individual in unsafe or unsupervised conditions. *See also* abuse.

nutrition   The sum of the processes by which one takes in and uses nutrients.

nutrition assessment   A comprehensive process for defining an individual's nutrition and hydration status using medical, nutrition, and medication intake histories, physical examination, anthropomorphic measurements, and laboratory data.

nutrition care   Interventions and counseling to promote appropriate nutrition and fluid intake, based on nutrition and hydration assessment and information about food, other sources of nutrients, and meal preparation consistent with the individual's cultural background and socioeconomic status. Nutrition therapy, a component of medical treatment, includes enteral and parenteral nutrition. *See also* nutrition.

nutrition screening   A process used to indicate the need for a nutritional assessment to determine whether a patient is malnourished or at risk for malnourishment.

patient   An individual who receives care, treatment, and services. For hospice providers, the patient and family are considered a single unit of care. Synonyms used by various health care fields include client, resident, customer, patient and family unit, consumer, and health care consumer.

performance improvement   The continuous study and adaptation of a health care organization's functions and processes to increase the probability of achieving desired outcomes and to better meet the needs of individuals and other users of services.

pharmacist   An individual who has a degree in pharmacy and is licensed and registered to prepare, preserve, compound, and dispense drugs and chemicals.

pharmacy   A licensed location where drugs are stored and dispensed.

physician   A doctor of medicine or doctor of osteopathy who, by virtue of education, training, and demonstrated competence, is granted clinical privileges by the organization to perform a specific diagnostic or therapeutic procedure(s) and who is fully licensed to practice medicine.

physician assistant   An individual who practices medicine with supervision by licensed physicians, providing patients with services ranging from primary medicine to specialized surgical care. The scope of practice is determined by state law, the supervising physician's delegation of responsibilities, the individual's education and experience, and the specialty and setting in which the individual works.

plan   A detailed method, formulated beforehand, that identifies needs, lists strategies to meet those needs, and sets goals and objectives. The format of the plan may include narratives, policies and procedures, protocols, practice guidelines, clinical paths, care maps, or a combination of these.

policies and procedures   The formal, approved description of how a governance, management, or clinical care process is defined, organized, and carried out.

program   An organized system of services designed to address the needs of the organization or individual.

protective services   A range of sociolegal, assistive, and remedial services that facilitate the exercise of individual rights and provide certain supportive and surrogate mechanisms. Such mechanisms are designed to help developmentally disabled individuals reach the maximum independence possible, yet protect them from exploitation, neglect, or abuse. Depending on the nature and extent of individual needs, protective services may range from counseling to full guardianship.

psychiatrist   A physician who specializes in assessing and treating persons having psychiatric disorders; is certified by the American Board of Psychiatry and Neurology or has the documented equivalent in education, training, or experience; and is fully licensed to practice medicine in the state in which he or she practices.

quality of care   The degree to which health services for individuals and populations increase the likelihood of desired health outcomes and are consistent with current professional knowledge. Dimensions of performance include the following: patient perspective issues; safety of the care environment; and accessibility, appropriateness, continuity, effectiveness, efficacy, efficiency, and timeliness of care.

registered nurse   An individual who is qualified by an approved postsecondary program or baccalaureate or higher degree in nursing and licensed by the state, commonwealth, or territory to practice professional nursing.

religion   The externals of one's belief system: church, prayers, traditions, rites, and rituals, among others.

safety   The degree to which the risk of an intervention (for example, use of a drug or a procedure) and risk in the care environment are reduced for a patient and other persons, including health care practitioners.

safety management   Activities selected and implemented by the organization to assess and control the impact of environmental risk, and to improve general environmental safety.

spirituality   An inner belief system. It is a delicate "spirit-to-spirit" relationship to oneself and others, and the God of one's understanding.

staff   Individuals, such as employees, contractors, or temporary agency personnel, who provide services in the organization.

staffing effectiveness   The number, competence, and skill mix of staff as related to the provision of needed services.

Index

A

B

C